WENDY HUTTON   PHOTOGRAPHY BY LUCA INVERNIZZI TETTONI

THE FOOD OF
MALAYSIA

62 Delicious Recipes from the Crossroads of Asia

Recipes by the chefs of **Bon Ton Restaurant, Kuala Lumpur**
and **Jonkers Restaurant, Malacca**
Styling by **Christina Ong**

TUTTLE Publishing
Tokyo | Rutland, Vermont | Singapore

CONTENTS

FOOD IN MALAYSIA

Where Asia's Greatest Cuisines Meet And Mingle

The Asian continent, encompassing the world's highest mountains, vast sandy deserts, millions of hectares of fertile rice fields, massive river deltas and tangled jungles, comes to its end in the peninsula known poetically to the ancient Greeks as the Golden Khersonese.

This golden land, the Malay Peninsula, lies where the monsoons meet and, over the centuries, saw sailing ships arriving from the west from Arabia, India and, much later on, from Europe. From the east came Chinese junks, Siamese vessels and the inter-island sailing craft of the Buginese and Javanese from the Indonesian archipelago.

The original people of the peninsula—known collectively as Orang Asli and now numbering less than 100,000—consist of about 20 different tribes belonging to two distinct linguistic groups. Later arrivals, who spread south from China and began settling in Malaysia around 4,000 years ago, were the ancestors of today's dominant group, the Malays.

The Malay kingdom of Malacca was the greatest port in the east during its heyday in the 15th century. By then, Malacca's sultan had embraced Islam, brought by Indian Muslim traders, and the new religion gradually spread throughout the peninsula.

The lives of the Muslim Malays were to change during the 19th century when the British began, first in Penang, then in Malacca, to gain control over the Malay states. The British brought in huge numbers of Chinese and Indian workers, dramatically altering not only the ethnic and social structure of the country but its eating habits as well.

In 1963, the Federation of Malaysia was formed, with the states of the peninsula combining with the Borneo states of Sabah and Sarawak. Malaysia's cuisines are as varied as its people. The Malays, Chinese and Indians continue to create their own foods, while cross-cultural borrowing in the kitchen has led to a number of uniquely 'Malaysian' dishes.

Then there is Nonya cuisine, the food of the Straits-born Chinese, combining both Malay and Chinese elements. It is arguably the most distinctive in the country.

The Eurasians, too—especially those of Portuguese origin in Malacca—have brought some of their traditional dishes, like Devil's Curry, and developed their own unique culinary blend in Malaysia, whipping up dishes such as Portuguese Otak Otak.

The Malaysian kitchen bustles with creativity. The nation's cooks lay claim to dishes such as the popular Black Pepper Crab and Butter Prawns. Malaysians

OPPOSITE: Traditionally built of wood and *atap* (thatch), Malay houses show subtle differences in design throughout Malaysia. Malaccan homes often feature beautiful tiles, reminiscent of their Portuguese heritage. **ABOVE:** Rice fields, an indelible part of the Malaysian landscape, nestle at the base of Sabah's majestic Mount Kinabalu, the highest peak in Southeast Asia, at 4,101 metres (13,455 feet), and growing.

love food, whether it's enjoyed at home with family and friends, eaten at food stalls or restaurants, or as part of a festive celebration. We invite you to join the feast: *Selamat makan*!

A Land Where Nature Smiles

Malaysia seems to have been blessed by nature, which saves volcanic eruptions, typhoons and lashing monsoon rains and floods for other parts of Asia.

Covering both the tip of the Asian peninsula and the northwestern part of Borneo, Malaysia, not surprisingly, varies in terrain and climate. The 'typical' lush tropical landscape—emerald green rice paddies, golden beaches fringed by groves of coconut palms—exists, but it is only part of the picture.

To the far north of the peninsula, near the Thai border, the climate is often dry and the landscape of endless paddy fields (for this is the 'rice bowl' of Malaysia) is relieved by abrupt limestone hills.

Much of the lush alluvial plain of the peninsula's west coast is planted with oil palm and rubber. This is ideal land for orchards too, and luscious tropical fruits such as the highly prized (and powerful smelling) durian, mangosteen, starfruit, furry red rambutans, *langsat* and other delights are grown here.

Contrasting with this, high on the Banjaran Titiwangsa, which is the main mountain range, the temperate climate of the Cameron Highlands makes it perfect not only for holiday-makers but for the tea plantations and market gardens which provide much of the fresh produce for Malaysian markets. Malaysians can thus vary typical tropical vegetables (such as water spinach, or *kangkung*, bamboo shoot, eggplant, okra, sweet potato and taro yam) with temperate-climate vegetables like cabbage, carrots, broccoli and peppers.

The generally muddy coastal waters of the Malacca Straits on the west coast are ideal for crabs and shellfish, the mangrove swamps providing an important breeding ground for prawns and other marine life. The east coast, washed by the South China Sea, provides not only postcard-perfect beaches but also ideal fishing grounds and countless small *kampung* (villages) along the coast make their livelihood from the sea.

Some 500 kilometres (300 miles) or so across this sea lie Sarawak and Sabah, characterized by traditional lifestyles and limited roads, especially in Sarawak, where rivers are still the major highways. Market produce is grown locally on a small scale in

Malaysia's long coastline is lined with traditional Malay fishing villages whose inhabitants have made their living from the seas for many centuries.

Sarawak, where many inland peoples still rely largely on wild edible plants.

Although most of the populated areas of Sarawak are low-lying, Sabah, by contrast, has a mountain range that culminates in Southeast Asia's tallest peak, Mount Kinabalu (4,100 metres, 13,450 feet). The local Dusun people living here grow 'hill' (non-irrigated) rice, pineapples and bananas on the steep slopes of the Crocker Range, while dozens of market gardens around Kundasang (approximately 1,500 metres/4,920 feet) grow a tremendous range of temperate-climate produce, including asparagus and mushrooms. Nearby, a dairy farm of contented Friesians produces a large percentage of the state's milk, and there is also a tea plantation.

With such a variety of locally produced vegetables, fruits, seafood and poultry to choose from, Malaysians have few limits on what they can create in the kitchen. The exception to this is that pork is forbidden to Muslims so it is never eaten by Malays and Indian Muslims.

A number of hotel restaurants, in deference to Muslim customers, substitute 'turkey ham' or 'beef bacon' for the real thing, and omit all pork dishes from their menu.

Seafood is very popular, and not just among the Malays and other coastal people. There is a superb array of fresh fish and a variety of shellfish such as prawns, squid, crabs, lobsters, as well as dried prawns and salted fish, not forgetting small dried anchovies, used for making *belachan* (dried prawn paste), the ingredient that gives an added 'kick' to many Malay, Nonya and Chinese dishes.

Most of the beef and mutton consumed locally is imported (often 'on the hoof' so that it can be slaughtered according to Muslim dietary laws), while the Chinese raise pigs for pork, their favourite meat.

Each ethnic group in Malaysia has its own way of transforming nature's bounty, which can come slathered with spices or subtly simple, rich in coconut milk gravy or bathed in a piquant sauce. Malaysians vary widely in their food preferences, and it is almost impossible to make generalizations on what they eat. For example, everyone's staple food is rice. But then again, noodles are widely eaten at breakfast, lunch and dinner! Perhaps the only universal quality is Malaysian food's irresistible flavour, be it Malay satay, pungent Indian mutton soup, Nonya chicken curry fragrant with lime leaves, Chinese pepper crab or Eurasian saltfish and pineapple curry.

THE GOLDEN KHERSONESE
Malay Cuisine Goes Global

For generations, during the time when Malaysia was known as the Golden Khersonese, the Malays lived a life relatively undisturbed by outside traders and invaders. Dwelling along the coasts or riverbanks, they enjoyed a largely peaceable existence, untroubled by the wars, famines and plagues that beset many other countries of the Asian continent.

In the last 2,000 years, intense sea trade between India and the Malay Archipelago resulted in the spread of Hinduism and intermarriages between the indigenous Malays and the Tamils and Gujeratis, especially in the coastal regions in the south. Around this time, up in the north, intermarriages with the Thai were common. Perhaps not surprisingly, these external influences nurtured a cuisine that was eclectic and exotic in style and taste.

Fish were abundant, rice grew in the paddies, wild and cultivated fruits and vegetables were available year-round in the constant climate. Fragrant herbs grew effortlessly, as did the indispensable coconut. Traditional meals were based on rice, with fish, vegetables and chilli-based sambals to add extra zing.

Travelling along today's highways that cross the peninsula from north to south and east to west, it comes as a surprise to learn that until well into the 20th century, travel through what was a largely jungle-covered land was very limited. As a result, regional styles of cuisine developed in different parts of the Malay Peninsula.

Given the history of Malaysia, it is understandable that the northern states of Kedah, Perlis and Kelantan, all of which border on Thailand, and Trengganu, which rubs shoulders with Kelantan, show distinct Thai influences in their cuisine. So, too, does Penang. A tangy and fragrant sourness is often added by the use of tamarind, sour carambola and limes, while fiery hot chillies so often present in Thai food are also popular in the northern Malaysian states.

Fresh herbs are frequently used to give a special touch to northern dishes. In addition to the herbs commonly used throughout Malaysia—lemongrass, pandanus leaf, the fra-

Local markets are filled with a bewildering variety of fresh and dried produce. The Central Market in the northeastern town of Kota Bahru is renowned for its wide variety of fresh herbs, often used to make Nasi Ulam or Kerabu.

grant leaf of the kaffir lime and the pungent polygonum or *daun kesum*—northern chefs include a type of basil that is very popular in Thailand known as *daun kemanggi*, leaves of a number of rhizomes, such as turmeric and zedoary (known locally as *cekur* or *kencur*), and the wonderfully fragrant wild ginger bud.

A popular northern dish, Nasi Ulam or Kerabu, consists of rice cooked with pandanus, galangal, lemongrass and kaffir lime leaves, and mixed with as many fresh herbs as can be found in the garden or market. In another rendition of this herb rice dish, a platter of fresh herbs, or *ulam*, is served with a spicy chilli sauce, rice and other cooked dishes.

Settled largely by the Minangkabau people from West Sumatra, the central state of Negeri Sembilan reflects its history in its food, with richly spiced dishes cooked in lashings of coconut milk—the popular dish, Rendang, being a perfect example. Likewise, Indonesian influences have infiltrated the kitchens throughout the Malaysian hinterland through migration; historical documents dating to the early 20th century show the influx of migrants from Sumatra to the tin mines in Kuala Lumpur. Nasi Padang—another universally popular Malaysian meal of rice served with vegetables and spicy meat, fish or poultry—comes from Padang, a district in West Sumatra. The Malay cuisine of Johore, in the far south, includes a number of Javanese influences, as groups of Javanese settled here over the past couple of centuries.

Largely isolated from the rest of the peninsula until well into the 20th century, the state of Pahang, with its dramatic jungled mountains and gorgeous sandy beaches, offers a relatively simple cuisine dominated by fresh, succulent seafood—its Ikan Bakar, or grilled fish, is a must-try.

Other states of Peninsular Malaysia tend to be more multiracial in character, and the indigenous Malay food is less distinctive than that of other areas.

Despite the regional differences, Malay food can be described as spicy and flavourful, although this does not necessarily mean

Food stalls throughout the country are very well-known for inexpensive home-cooked food. Nasi Campur (mixed rice) allows diners to pick and choose from a variety of cooked Malay-style dishes which are eaten with rice.

TAMAN RESTORAN
10

NASI HIDANG, CHAMPOR, GORING,
MEE DAN BIHOON, GORING, HAILAM,
BANDONG SOOP, ROJAK

ASAM LAKSA NASI AYAM

NASI CAMPUR & HIDANG

There is no dearth of eating places in Malaysia, and one way of combating direct competition between stall holders is to serve complementary foods, making Malaysia the perfect place for a satisfying "food crawl". In the photo, the stall on the right offers rice served with side dishes, whereas the stall on the left provides the perfect complements of soups and drinks.

chilli-hot. But you can rest assured that even if the main dishes are not hot, there'll be a chilli-based sambal on hand.

Coconuts and Spice and all Things Nice

Nobody who has sat under the stars on a warm tropical night and smelled the tantalizing fragrance of Satay—tiny spiced kebabs—sizzling over charcoal at a nearby food stall can resist Malay food.

The magic in Malay cuisine lies in its spices and herbs. Traditional Southeast Asian spices have been joined over the centuries by Indian, Middle Eastern and Chinese spices, so the partnership of coriander and cumin (the basis of many Malay 'curries') is joined by pepper, cardamom, star anise, and fenugreek—just to name a few of the many spices in the Malay cook's cupboard.

Food without seasoning is unthinkable—even a simple slice of fried fish is rubbed with turmeric powder and salt before cooking. Many of the seasonings that enhance Malay food are not dried spices but fragrant fresh roots, such as turmeric and galangal (*lengkuas*), and other 'wet' ingredients like chillies, onions and garlic. Fresh seasonings and dried spices are normally pounded to a fine paste and cooked gently in oil before liquid—either creamy coconut

milk or a sour broth—is added to the wok.

Food for the barbecue is also marinated, sometimes for days on end, or simmered in spices before cooking. Spices transform plain leftover white rice into a tasty Nasi Goreng— first fry pounded onions and chillies, then add the rice, giving it a quick stir-fry until fragrant.

Fish has always played an important part in the Malay diet, and in Malaysian food, it appears in the form of *ikan bilis* (tiny dried anchovies) and dried prawns, added for flavour. And then there is *belachan* (dried prawn paste) which, despite its pungent odour when raw and during cooking, gives an irresistible extra flavour to countless dishes.

These days, many of the seasonings and sauces used in Malaysian dishes are available in cans and packets in local and overseas supermarkets, and pre-packed sachets of spice mixtures make cooking soups a breeze. Although these pre-mixed concoctions do not taste as authentic as the real thing, for the busy Malaysian housewife, they are acceptable substitutes.

Malaysian Feasts

Malaysia is modernizing rapidly, and more and more of its people are moving into terraced or semi-

Malaysia's much-loved cartoonist, Lat, remembers his childhood (and food) in the *kampung*.

We had two choices for breakfast: boiled bananas or boiled tapioca. Perfect when either one is dipped in grated coconut mixed with white sugar.

Fooh! Foooh!

Fooh! Fooh!

LAT.

detached houses with minimal gardens. The traditional *kampung* (village) house set in a cleanly swept yard shaded by coconuts, bananas and other fruit trees, with chickens pecking their way around a variety of kitchen herbs and vegetables, is increasingly something of the past.

Modern urban lifestyles leave little time for gardening or preparing complex dishes. Adding to the inertia is the perpetual sale on food in Malaysia. From the charming roadside stalls packed with fresh fruit and drink, noodle soups and fried fritters, and the eating houses offering authentic Malaysian Chinese, Indian or Malay fare, to the restaurants offering French, African and other exotic cuisine in larger cities, whatever takes your fancy, you name it and chances are, you will find it—cheap and good.

The *kenduri* (feast) is the one occasion when home-style Malay cuisine comes into its own. These feasts are held during special festivals such as weddings and Hari Raya (the Day of Celebration) that marks the end of Ramadan (the Holy Month of Fasting). To prepare for a *kenduri*, all the women in the family or village take out their biggest cooking pots and work for several days virtually through the night, scraping and squeezing coconuts for milk,

pounding mountains of shallots, garlic, chillies and spices, cutting and chopping, simmering and stirring, until they have cooked up an impressive array of fish curries, *gulais* (spicy soups) of vegetables bathed in coconut milk and seasoned perhaps with fresh prawns, coconut-rich Rendang, tingling hot prawn sambals, and a colourful array of desserts. The whole family helps out. Neighbours are expected to chip in too, according to the unspoken agreement that all feasts in the village are communal events, and that they will receive the same help when it is their turn to hold a *kenduri*.

Although it occurs infrequently, the *kenduri* is such an important part of the village culture of Malaysia that Malaysian students in foreign universities have been known to organize their own *kenduri* get-togethers, thus attesting to the bonding influence of food on the everyday Malaysian.

With their innate courtesy and hospitality, the Malays consider it an honour to be able to invite any fortunate passer-by to join in the *kenduri*. Traditionally, women sit separately from the men, while babies crawl about or swing in a sarong cradle nearby. Children either peek shyly at the guest or race about happily—after, of course, enjoying the sumptuous feast that shows Malay cuisine at its best.

MALAYSIA'S CULINARY MELTING POT

An Exchange of Cultural Food Styles

Some may say that the closest Malaysians have to a national dish is Nasi Lemak—fragrant rice cooked in coconut milk, and served with fried egg, Sambal Belachan and crispy fried fish. Yet others think the Malaysian Rojak best encapsulates what is most unique about Malaysia's cuisine: *rojak* is a mixed salad of sliced fruits, vegetables and bean curd tossed in a spicy peanut sauce, sometimes with a touch of prawn paste. Incidentally, *rojak* in local slang refers to a haphazard mixture of things. And what would you expect from a place that is teeming with multi-cultural influences, history and die-hard foodies?

Celestial Cuisines in Nanyang

Gas jets spurt like fire-breathing dragons, engulfing huge cast-iron woks where a mass of noodles is being tossed, seasoned and scooped by a perspiring Chinese chef. This is a scene re-enacted at food stalls and restaurants throughout Malaysia, where Chinese cuisine has become an inseparable part of the magical Malaysian mix.

When Chinese merchants sailed their junks across the South China Sea, visiting the ports of north Borneo before lengthy trading sessions in Malacca, they set in motion a process that was to have a profound influence on the region.

Nanyang, the lands across the Great Southern Ocean, became renowned as a source of exotic ingredients and wealth. A few of these Chinese traders stayed on in the Malay Peninsula, often marrying local women and forming the beginnings of Peranakan or Straits-Chinese culture. However, it was not until the arrival of the British colonials in Singapore in 1819 that the stage was set for a huge wave of migration.

Thousands of Chinese workers poured into Singapore, and as tin was discovered in the Malay Peninsula, many moved north to areas like Penang, Malacca, Kuala Lumpur and Taiping. Others headed straight for the gold mines and coalfields of Sarawak, or moved to British North Borneo (now Sabah) to work the land. More came later to labour in rubber plantations that soon altered the landscape and economy of the country. The Chinese brought with them the cooking styles of their homeland, mostly the southern provinces of Guangdong and Fujian, introducing the indigenous people of the Malay Peninsula and northern Borneo to a range of ingredients now used by every ethnic group in Malaysia: noodles, bean sprouts, tofu and soy sauce. Their technique of stir-frying small portions of food

OPPOSITE: Although time-consuming, the effort put into the subtle details of a Nonya feast, either for a festive or a simple meal, is the key to a rewarding culinary experience.
ABOVE: Food stalls serve customers who perch on often rickety stools to enjoy an al fresco meal and those who buy take-away food to enjoy at home or work.

Diners in these open-air eating houses may not enjoy the fully air-conditioned comfort of a restaurant, but the food is usually cheaper and just as delicious.

in a little oil over very high heat in a conical frying pan called a wok was also widely adopted. In turn, Malaysia's Chinese developed a penchant for spices and chillies—any local Chinese coffee shop or restaurant will offer pickled green chillies, or red chilli sambal to enliven noodles and rice-based meals. The Malaysian Chinese borrowed curry leaves from the Indians, experimented with English condiments like Worcestershire and tomato sauce, and added Indian and Malay spices to the cooking pot.

Almost any self-respecting Chinese cook can whip up a tasty Malay-style chicken or fish curry, and most versions of laksa (a spicy noodle soup) are prepared by the Chinese. They're not averse to enjoying a number of Indian dishes too, especially some of the pungent fish curries and Indian breads, such as Roti Canai and murtabak.

Chinese food is widely accepted as one of the world's greatest cuisines. One of its hallmarks is the ingenious use of ingredients—the Chinese chef's ability to transform 'spare parts' into a dish that tastes like an exotic luxury is virtually legendary. The Chinese also place great importance on the contrast of colours, textures and flavours, both within a dish and the overall meal.

The light, clean, non-greasy food of the Cantonese, and the pungent, chilli-hot cuisine of Sichuan are well-known abroad, with northern cuisine

from Peking also attracting a following. Although Cantonese is the dominant dialect group in Malaysia, there are large numbers of Hokkien, Teochew, Hockchew from Foochow, Hakka, Hainanese and Henghua people, often concentrated in a particular town or region, each with its own style of cooking.

All this means that although Chinese cuisine in Malaysia seems somehow familiar, it's also full of delicious surprises. Like the fiery punch of crabs fried with black pepper, chillies, fermented soybean paste and curry leaves, or the smooth texture of fresh rice noodles (kway teow) fried with prawns, egg and bean sprouts. Malaysian Chinese—who enjoy their food so enthusiastically that one might almost wonder if they live to eat rather than eat to live—dine out frequently, at roadside stalls and in simple open-fronted coffee shops as well as more formal restaurants.

As many visitors have noted, Malaysia's Chinese always seem to be eating. After a light breakfast (maybe Western-style toast or perhaps noodles or steamed tidbits known as dim sum), they make room for a mid-morning snack, which could be Indian Curry Puffs or sweet Malay cake. Lunch would most likely be noodles or rice with Chinese, Malay or Indian side dishes, and dinner, a formal Cantonese meal, a vast spread of seafood at a restaurant, a family meal of rice, soup, vegetables and meat or seafood, or even Western fast-food. And before bedtime, they man-

age to squeeze in just one more bowl of noodles or perhaps some fried bananas. With so many good things to eat, who can possibly limit themselves to just three meals a day?

Spicy Indian Soul Mates

Visitors to Malaysia, noting the many Indian Muslim food stalls, Indian 'banana leaf' restaurants and the universal popularity of the pancake-like Indian bread, Roti Canai, might be surprised to learn that the Indian community makes up only about 10 percent of the nation's population.

Indian cuisines—especially those from the south, where most of Malaysia's Indians originated—share some similarities with Malay cuisine in their generous use of spices and coconut, so it took little encouragement for Indian food to catch on. And it's not just the easy-to-love flavours of Indian food that make it widely popular; Malay Muslims can rest assured that Muslim dietary laws will be observed in Indian Muslim restaurants.

Like their Chinese counterparts, Indian traders have been recorded in the region for more than a thousand years, but it was only in the 19th century that they came to Malaya in large numbers.

Most were brought in as contract labourers to work on the rubber estates, where miniature Indian villages complete with temples, schools and toddy

shops sprung up. Others came to work on the railways or in setting up the telecommunications network, while many Indian Muslims opened restaurants, textile shops or small sundry shops.

Although Malaysia has small communities of Sikhs from the Punjab region in India and Malayalees from Kerala, the overwhelming majority in the southwest are Tamils from the southeastern state of Tamil Nadu (once Madras). Indian vegetarian food is justifiably popular in Malaysia. Southern vegetarian dishes are cleverly spiced—brown mustard seeds, black gram *dhal*, curry leaves and dried chillies make one popular spice combination—and are often combined with coconut milk or freshly grated coconut for extra flavour. Cereals are also a common ingredient; the Indian steamed bread (*idli*) and the finest, crispiest pancake imaginable (*dosai*) are made from ground black gram *dhal* and rice.

Traditionally, the typical Hindu vegetarian meal of *dhal*, several spicy vegetable dishes with a mound of rice, a glass of thin spicy soup (*resam*), hot sour pickle and yogurt are served on the ultimate disposable plate: a rectangular piece of freshly washed banana leaf. Some Indian Muslim restaurants caught up with the idea and are now offering their robust fare, with spicy dry mutton, crab curry, prawns, fried fish and other dishes as well as vegetables on a banana leaf. Today, many of these restaurants simply advertise

Cylindrical containers made of stainless steel, held in place with an ingeniously designed metal handle—the tiffin carrier is an Indian invention that found its way into the Nonya kitchen.

'banana leaf curry', meaning, of course, you eat what's spread on the leaf rather than the leaf itself.

India's most spectacular contribution to the Malaysian culinary scene is Roti Canai (literally 'flattened bread'). This is an adaptation of Roti Paratha, traditionally made with a mixture of white and whole wheat flour. The Malaysian version combines pure white flour, ghee and—the secret touch—a little evaporated or condensed milk for an extra light dough, which is then kneaded and rolled into balls and left to stand.

Then comes the dramatic part: the ball of dough is punched flat and then grasped at the edge and swung around in ever increasing circles to make a paper-thin pancake. This is then flattened, shaped and fried in ghee to a golden brown. Some theatrical *roti* makers will even throw the cooked bread into the air with a flourish before chopping it, karate fashion, with the edge of the hands.

Finally, the Roti Canai arrives crisp and crunchy, accompanied by bowls of curry sauce or *dhal*. Fill the dough with chopped onion and minced mutton or chicken before frying it, and the resulting stuffed pancake becomes a *murtabak*, a satisfying meal in itself.

Malaysia's Indian hawkers have created unique versions of several local dishes, preparing foods you'd never find in India. Indian Mee Goreng, for example, combines fresh yellow Hokkien noodles, tofu, bean sprouts and *belachan*. Another noodle dish is the Indian version of Mee Siam (itself a Malay version of a Thai-style noodle dish). And then there's Indian Rojak, vegetables and deep-fried fritters with a sweet sauce, totally different from the Malay and Nonya versions.

Indian Curry Puffs—folded pastry with a spicy potato filling—have been adopted enthusiastically by the Malays and Chinese, who create their own versions, sometimes adding pieces of cooked egg and chicken in a superb shortcrust pastry deep-fried to a melt-in-the-mouth texture.

Rich Indian mutton or lamb soup is another universal food-stall favourite, while Indian curries featuring chicken or fish are popular throughout Malaysia.

Nonya cuisine—the "food of love"

Until about a decade ago, Malaysia's unique and arguably most delicious cuisine was in danger of disappearing. Fortunately for lovers of fine food, growing awareness of Malaysia's diverse heritage and a desire to preserve it seem to have saved the cuisine of the Nonyas. An increasing number of restaurants now feature Nonya cuisine, and the printing of Nonya recipes in books and magazines means that enthusiastic cooks of any ethnic background can reproduce this cuisine at home.

Tracing their descent from the Portuguese who ruled Malacca during the 16th century, these dancers decked out in ethnic garb entertain in the Portuguese Settlement.

The so-named Straits-born Chinese, descendants of early settlers in Penang and Malacca, combine elements of both Chinese and Malay culture, quite unlike the mass of Chinese migrants who arrived around the turn of this century and up until the 1930s.

These pioneering Chinese traders, many of whom became wealthy men, took Malay wives, although as time went on, children of these early mixed marriages generally married pure Chinese or the children of other Straits Chinese, thus greatly diluting any Malay blood they may have had.

The women, known as *nonyas*, and the men, *babas*, generally spoke a mixture of Malay and Chinese dialect, dressed in modified Malay style, and combined the best of both cuisines in the kitchen.

Typical Chinese ingredients (such as tofu, soy sauce, preserved soybeans, black prawn paste, sesame seeds, dried mushrooms and dried lily buds) blended beautifully with Malay herbs, spices and fragrant roots. Being non-Muslim, the Straits Chinese cooked pork dishes Malay style, and added distinctive local ingredients (coconut milk, spices and sour tamarind juice) to basic Chinese recipes. The Nonya pork satay, served with a spicy pineapple sauce, demonstrates perfectly this felicitous blending of styles.

Straits Chinese or Nonya cuisine often requires painstaking effort. In old-style households, the Nonya wife devoted all her time to running the home and supervising the kitchen, assisted by a small army of servants—a luxury few modern Malaysian women can indulge in. Another reason leading to the near-demise of Nonya cuisine is that today, many Nonya girls marry non-Straits-born Chinese, and therefore tend to cook the kind of food their Cantonese or Hokkien husbands are familiar with.

Distinct differences evolved between the cuisine of the Penang Nonyas and that of Malacca. In Penang, which is geographically much closer to Thailand, the Nonyas developed a passion for sour food (using lots of lime and tamarind juice), fiery hot chillies, fragrant herbs and pungent black prawn paste.

Malacca Nonyas prepare food that is generally rich in coconut milk and Malay spices (such as coriander and cumin), and they a have to tendency to add more sugar than their northern counterparts.

Fruits and vegetables—once gathered fresh from the garden—are prepared in imaginative ways by the Nonyas. Unripe jackfruit, the heart of the banana bud, sweet potato leaves and tiny sour *belimbing* fruits are all transformed in the kitchen. The back garden also yielded the herbs that make Nonya food so aromatic: the kaffir lime leaf, pungent *laksa* leaf or polygonum, the camphor-smelling leaf of the root, zedoary, fresh turmeric leaves and fragrant pandanus.

Nonya cakes are renowned for their richness and variety. Most are based on Malay recipes, using inexpensive and easily available ingredients such as freshly grated tapioca root, sweet potato, *agar agar*, gelatin, glutinous rice, palm sugar and coconut milk, with additional flavouring from the pandanus leaf.

Little touches often transform an already delicious dish, such as the Malay favourite, glutinous 'black' rice. Nonya cooks usually add a few 'dragon's eyes', dried longan fruits, for an elusive smoky flavour.

Eurasian Food—When East Meets West

What sort of food would you expect from a Catholic cook living in Malaysia, whose ancestors were Portuguese, Malay, Javanese and Indian? To find the answer, head for Malacca, the historic town on Peninsular Malaysia's west coast, just 150 kilometres (100 miles) from the capital, Kuala Lumpur.

When the sultanate of Malacca fell to Portuguese invaders in 1511, the new rulers sought to establish control by encouraging Portuguese soldiers to marry local girls, and by bringing a number of Portuguese girls to marry local men.

Portuguese rule ended more than 350 years ago, yet in the so-called Portuguese Settlement of Malacca, families have names such as Da Silva, Dias and Sequeira, and many of the people speak Cristao, a Portuguese-based dialect.

Today, the names and the Catholic faith are the only things Portuguese about Malacca's Eurasian community. In other parts of Malaysia, the children of cross-cultural marriages during the 19th and 20th centuries, where one parent was most commonly English or Dutch, blend into Malaysian society, and there are no enclaves of these Eurasians such as the one in Malacca.

Naturally, the mixed heritage of Malaysia's Eurasians has produced a fascinating cuisine with many excellent dishes. Cooks of Portuguese descent are renowned for using generous amounts of spices, particularly in such dishes like Devil's Curry, an adaptation of Goanese *vindaloo* where vinegar and chillies vie for attention.

Perhaps the most striking characteristic of Eurasian cooks in Malaysia and elsewhere is their

Eurasian stews are given a Malaysian twist with Malay herbs combined with Indian brown mustard, vinegar, a paste of freshly pounded chilies and a Chinese favourite, cut belly pork. **PAGES 20–21:** A mouth-watering variety of fresh produce gives Malaysian cooks an endless array of options.

One of the most popular Nonya dishes among Malaysians of any background is *laksa*, a rice-noodle soup that blends Malay seasonings with Chinese noodles. The Malacca Nonya version is rich in coconut milk, its basic spice paste made from dried prawns, fresh turmeric, chillies, *belachan*, lemongrass and galangal (*lengkuas*).

You can tell a true Penang Nonya *laksa* from just one look and whiff of its fragrance. It uses almost all the spice paste ingredients of the Malacca version, then adds the fragrant bud of the wild ginger, *laksa* leaf, pungent prawn paste, shredded pineapple and raw onion, and drenches the lot with a tamarind-sour gravy with no coconut milk added.

readiness to borrow ingredients from other cultures. English or Dutch-style dishes are transformed from innocuous stews to distinctly Eurasian dishes with the addition of oyster or soy sauce, a handful of spices, green chillies and sour tamarind juice.

The Cuisines of Borneo—Feasts from the Jungle

Smoked wild boar stir-fried with freshly-cut bamboo shoots, braised fern tips plucked from the jungle, sweet juicy clams fried with a slathering of chillies and herbs, and raw fish salad drenched with lime juice. These are just some of the delights emanating from the kitchens of Malaysian Borneo, and the list goes on.

Sabah and Sarawak are peopled by a bewilder-ing range of ethnic groups, each having their own culinary specialities. The influx of Chinese immigrants during the 19th and early 20th centuries led to the adoption of certain Chinese cooking styles, especially stir-frying, and seasonings such as soy sauce, now a permanent fixture in almost every kitchen.

More recently, since the formation of Malaysia in 1963, the arrival of Indians, Malays and Chinese from Peninsular Malaysia has further influenced local styles so that today, traditional Borneo dishes are generally found only in the longhouses and remote villages of the interior, or in isolated coastal settlements.

Naturally, the diet of the people living along the estuaries and coastline is dominated by seafood, and as the majority of coastal people are Muslim, pork is never eaten. Inland folk, predominantly non-Muslim, enjoy whatever can be caught in the rivers or forest, such as wild pig, deer and other jungle game.

Rice, especially 'hill' rice grown in non-irrigated fields, is the favourite staple, although in some areas, a starchy porridge made from the sago palm is still enjoyed on occasion. The semi-nomadic Penan of Sarawak are well-known for their regular harvesting of the sago palm, as are the Bisaya of southwest Sabah, while some hill tribes such as Sabah's Muruts make a similar porridge from tapioca roots.

People in the remote parts of Sabah and Sarawak have developed ways of preserving food, an essen-tial art in the absence of refrigeration, either through

These villagers share a common but unique meal in Borneo's rainforest, where lengths of fresh bamboo—the ubiquitous utensil of the jungle—are packed with raw, soaked sticky rice and meat, and steamed over a fire.

smoking or curing chunks of raw pork or fish with salt and cooked rice over several months. The flavour of this cured delicacy is, to say the least, challenging to the uninitiated.

Although cooking styles vary, the general trend is for coastal cuisines to be more 'Malay' in their use of spices and coconut milk. The tribes living further inland make use of the abundance of wild vegetables (including several types of edible fern), herbs and sour fruits. Dried fish, dried prawns and dried prawn paste are popular seasonings throughout Sabah and Sarawak, as they are in Peninsular Malaysia.

THE MALAYSIAN KITCHEN
Tips for Cooking Malaysian Dishes

Contrary to popular belief, you don't need a range of exotic implements to cook Malaysian food. Most of the utensils found in the average Western kitchen can be adapted, although there are several items which will make preparation and cooking a great deal easier.

First and foremost is something to grind or crush the *rempah* or spice paste, the mixture of seasonings such as chillies, shallots and spices used to season many dishes. The rhythmic thump, thump, thump of a granite mortar and pestle is a familiar sound throughout the country, yet it requires effort, time and expertise to produce a beautifully smooth *rempah*, and the proper type of mortar and pestle is difficult to find abroad.

Many modern Malaysian cooks use a small blender, spice grinder similar to a coffee grinder or food processor to deal with large amounts of ingredients, although the old faithful *batu lesung* is still kept for simple grinding tasks. (See Cooking Methods, page 24, for details on how to prepare *rempah*.)

A large, solid wooden chopping board—usually made from a cross section cut from a tree trunk—is used for a multitude of tasks, together with a solid cleaver with a blade about 3–4 inches (7½–10 cm) deep. Any Asian supplies store should stock this type of cleaver, which is far more effective at chopping up poultry, fish and crabs, and mincing meat than a normal kitchen knife.

For all types of Malaysian cooking, particularly Chinese, a wok (*kuali*) is essential. The shape of the conical wok distributes the heat evenly, while its sloping sides ensure that when you're stir-frying, food falls back into the pan and not out over the edge. It's also more practical for deep-frying, and allows the food to be cooked in less oil, and for the

Traditional kitchens such as this Nonya one in Malacca may look romantic, but most Malaysian cooks prefer today's modern Western appliances.

Claypot

Stone Mortar and Pestle

A stone mortar and pestle, is still indispensible in a traditional Malaysian kitchen for pounding smaller quantities of ingredients. The claypot is designed to go directly over a flame, and can also be used in an oven.

right amount of evaporation for dishes which begin with lots of liquid and finish with a trace of very thick sauce.

Choose a heavy wok (which is safer as it is less likely to tip over) in cast iron or specially treated steel. It is now possible to get woks with a non-stick surface which can be scraped with metal frying spatulas, unlike delicate Teflon-covered surfaces which can only be used with plastic ones. If you are using an electric stove, try to find a wok that has a flattened bottom, or failing that, use a special ring to hold the wok securely.

To season a new wok before using it, rub the inside surface with a cut onion, then heat a little oil and fry the onion gently for a few minutes. Discard the oil and onion, rinse the wok thoroughly with hot water and wipe it dry. Do not use abrasives and scourers on your wok; hot soapy water and a sponge should be sufficient.

A long-handled frying spatula for stir-frying, as well as a circular perforated ladle for lifting out deep-fried food, are essential partners to your wok. It should be noted that extremely high heat is needed when stir-frying food. Many electric stoves cannot achieve the ideal heat, and Malaysian cooks—especially Chinese Malaysian cooks—insist on at least one gas fire, often with a double ring of gas jets. If you are using an old-style electric stove which usually will not reach a very high heat and which cannot be quickly reduced in temperature, you might consider investing in a gas-fired ring to use with your wok.

Although by no means essential, a claypot, or earthenware *belanga*, is an attractive addition to your pots and pans. Before you use it, you might like to try the Malaysian trick of gently frying some grated coconut until it turns brown. Discard the coconut, wipe the pot with a cloth and store.

Steaming is another popular method of cooking. Chinese cooks traditionally used a bamboo steamer with a woven cover, placed over a wok a few inches above boiling water. Bamboo is an ideal material, as it absorbs the moisture that condenses on the cover and keeps it from falling back onto the food. If you are using a multi-tiered metal steamer—which many Malaysian cooks now do—a kitchen towel under the lid should do the trick.

Stores selling woks usually also sell perforated metal disks designed to sit above the water level inside a wok, so it can be used instead of a single-tiered steamer. You can put wrapped parcels of food directly on this, or, in the case of unwrapped food, on a plate set on the perforated disk. Cover the wok with a large domed lid and keep the water at a gentle simmer during steaming, topping up the water from time to time.

An electric rice cooker is a great boon if you're eating rice fairly often. It's foolproof, producing soft, fluffy rice every time, and also keeps rice warm for latecomers. Alternatively, use a heavy saucepan with a tight-fitting lid to steam your rice.

Fresh banana leaves are often used to wrap bundles of food for steaming or grilling, the leaf holding in the moisture and seasonings, and adding its subtle flavour to the food. A layer of parchment (not waxed) paper and another layer of aluminium foil or, if you prefer, just the foil—will make an adequate substitute.

A few less common kitchen tools are used for special dishes, although a little imagination will always produce substitutes. The four-spouted cup for making lacy Roti Jala pancakes can be replaced by a plastic squeeze bottle; a heavy cast iron skillet substitutes for the metal griddle or *tawa* used for Indian breads, and large ladles will do the task of special flat mesh baskets used to remove noodles from boiling water.

Cooking Methods

Malaysian cooks use a wide range of cooking methods—from pan-frying, deep-frying and stir-frying to braising, boiling, steaming and grilling over charcoal or under a grill.

It's essential to know how to prepare the *rempah* or basic seasoning paste required for many dishes. Before beginning, all the ingredients should be peeled and sliced. The principle is to grind or blend the toughest ingredients first, adding softer and wetter ingredients towards the end. Whether using a mortar and pestle, a blender or food processor, the order is the same. First grind any dried spices or nuts until fine, then add the other hard ingredients, such as lemongrass and galangal (already sliced or chopped in small pieces). Pound or process until fine, then add softer rhizomes, such as fresh turmeric and ginger, soaked dried chillies and sliced fresh chillies. When these are fine, add the ingredients that are full of moisture, such as sliced shallots and garlic, as well as soft prawn paste.

If you are using a food processor or blender, you will probably need to add just a little liquid to keep the blades turning. If the *rempah* is to be fried, add a little of the specified amount of cooking oil, and if it is to be cooked in coconut milk, add some of this. While processing, you will probably need to stop the machine frequently to scrape down the sides using a flat rubber spatula or long spoon. Try to avoid larger chunks of ingredients being left behind and not getting ground. Continue until you have a fine paste.

Some cooks add water rather than the cooking medium to the blender; this means that the *rempah* will need to be cooked for a longer period of time before adding the other ingredients, to allow the water to evaporate and the *rempah* to eventually fry rather than just stew.

The spice paste is generally gently fried before any other liquid is added. Malaysian cooks will tell you to cook the *rempah* 'until it smells fragrant' or 'until the oil comes out', both accurate descriptions of what happens after 3–5 minutes of frying over gentle heat, stirring frequently. The spice paste must be thoroughly cooked at this stage or the resulting dish will have a raw taste to it.

Coconut milk is often added to the basic spice paste, generally in two stages. The thinner coconut milk is added, a little at a time, to the cooked spice paste (often after pieces of meat or chicken have also been browned) and is stirred frequently, lifted with a ladle and poured back into the pan, until it comes to a boil. This process ensures the coconut milk does not curdle. The coconut gravy is then simmered gently, with the pan uncovered. The thick coconut milk or cream is added just before the dish is to be served, heated through but not boiled, to enrich and thicken the gravy or sauce.

LEFT: The bamboo steamer is an Asian kitchen classic. It consists of at least two round containers made of woven bamboo strips—more can be stacked on if needed—and a lid. Most cooks prefer to place the steamer in the wok over boiling water rather than over cold water, as this allows them more control over the cooking temperature. The food that needs the most thorough steaming is usually placed in the lowermost tier, and the food with the least heat needed, in the top tier. The woven bamboo allows the hot air to circulate and absorbs condensation, and is ideal for steaming *dim sum* items such as *pau* and *siew mai*. **RIGHT:** Walk into any grandmother's kitchen in Malaysia and you are likely to see this treasure trove of sauces, spices and dried foodstuff. Nowadays, with the increasingly fast-paced lifestyles of the young Malaysian women, canned food and pre-packed mixtures are replacing some of these more authentic ingredients.

AUTHENTIC MALAYSIAN INGREDIENTS

Asam gelugur is the Malay name for the sweet-sour garcinia fruit that resembles a dried apple. Dried slices of the fruit are used in place of tamarind pulp in some Malay and Nonya dishes.

Banana buds are the unopened flowers of the banana plant. They taste like artichokes and are a popular salad ingredient in Asia. To prepare, remove the coarse outer petals of the bud, quarter the tender heart and slice it lengthwise. If not using immediately, soak the slices in cold water or sprinkle lime juice over to prevent discolouration.

Banana leaves infuse a delicate flavour and aroma to food and are used as wrappers when steaming or grilling dishes, or as little trays to hold food when cooking. Soften the leaves slightly in boiling water before use to prevent them from cracking when folded.

Bangkuang is a root vegetable native to tropical America, where it is known as jicama. It is a crunchy mild tuber with a white flesh and beige skin that peels off easily. It is excellent eaten raw with a spicy dip, as in *rojak*, or cooked until soft, as in Popiah (page 42). Substitute daikon radish.

Bean sprouts (*taugeh*) normally found in Malaysia are sprouted green mung beans. Soybean sprouts, a larger variety, are also available but less common. Bean sprouts are excellent when lightly blanched and used as a crunchy topping or stir-fried with chives and sesame oil as a side dish. Purchase sprouts fresh as they lose their crisp texture quickly. They keep in the refrigerator, immersed in water, for a few days.

Belachan or dried prawn paste is a dense mixture of fermented ground prawns with a remarkably strong odour. It is sold in dried blocks that range in colour from pink to blackish brown. It should be roasted before use—either wrapped in foil and dry-roasted in a wok or skillet, or toasted over a gas flame on the back of a spoon—to enhance its flavour and kill bacteria. In some recipes, *belachan* is ground with the rest of the ingredients and then fried in oil without toasting. It is not to be confused with black prawn paste (*hay koh*) which tastes and smells different.

Belimbing is a pale green, acidic fruit about 5–7 cm (2–3 in) long, often added to curries, soups and pickles. It belongs to the same family as the starfruit and is sometimes called baby starfruit.

Black prawn paste (*hay koh*) is a black, pungent, molasses-like seasoning made of fermented prawns, salt, sugar and thickeners. It is used as a sauce or a dip. It is sometimes labelled as *petis* and is unrelated to *belachan*.

Candlenuts (*buah keras*) are waxy, cream-coloured nuts similar in size and texture to macadamia nuts, which can be used as a substitute (although less-expensive almonds or cashews will also do). They are never eaten raw, but are chopped, ground and cooked with other seasonings and added to Malay and Nonya curries and spice mixtures for flavour and texture. They go rancid quickly because of their high oil content, so buy small packets and keep them refrigerated.

Cardamom pods are used to perfume rice dishes, curries, cakes and desserts—giving foods a heady, sweet scent. Fibrous, straw-coloured pods enclose 15–20 pungent, black seeds. The pods should be first bruised lightly with a cleaver or a pestle when used whole. It is better to buy whole pods instead of seeds. Do not buy ground cardamom as it is virtually flavourless compared to cardamom pods.

Dried chillies

Fresh red chillies

Bird's-eye chillies

Chillies are indispensable in Asian cooking. The most commonly used fresh green and red Asian finger chillies are moderately hot. Tiny red, green or yellow-orange *chili padi* or bird's-eye chillies are used in some dishes and sambals, and are very hot, designed for strong palates. **Dried chillies** are usually cut into lengths and soaked in warm water to soften before use. Dried chillies have a very different flavour from fresh ones. To reduce the heat, discard some or all of the seeds before preparing. **Chilli powder** is a hot seasoning made from ground dried chillies.

Chinese celery is often referred to as "local" celery in Malaysia. The stems are very slender and more fragrant than normal celery—more of a herb than a vegetable. The leaves are generously used to garnish a variety of Chinese dishes. Substitute celery leaves or Italian parsley.

Chinese plum sauce is a reddish-brown condiment made from salted plums, vinegar, sugar and a dash of chillies. Sold in jars or cans in supermarkets, it is used as a dip for spring rolls.

Cockles (*hum*) are tiny shellfish that are also known as blood cockles or blood clams. They are usually very briefly blanched or fried in Fried Kway Teow (page 72). Cockles are known to carry hepatitis, so be careful where you buy them and cook thoroughly.

Coconut is used in many dishes in Malaysia in much the same way that milk or cream are used in Western cooking. **Coconut cream** and **milk** are made by squeezing the flesh of freshly grated mature coconuts. To obtain **coconut cream**, about ½ cup (125 ml) water is added for each grated coconut, then squeezed and strained. **Thick coconut milk** is obtained by adding 1 cup (250 ml) of water to the grated coconut, then pressing it to extract the juice. **Thin coconut milk** is obtained by adding another 2 cups (500 ml) of water to the already squeezed grated coconut and pressing it a second time. Although freshly pressed cream and milk have more flavour, they are now widely sold canned and in packets which are quick, convenient and quite tasty. Canned or packet coconut cream or milk comes in varying consistencies depending on the brand, and you will need to try them out and adjust the thickness by adding water as needed. In general, you should add 1 cup (250 ml) water to 1 cup (250 ml) canned or packet coconut cream to obtain thick coconut milk, and 2 cups (500 ml) water to 1 cup (250 ml) coconut cream to obtain thin coconut milk. These mixing ratios are only general guides and you should adjust the consistency to individual taste.

Coriander is a pungent herb and spice plant that is essential in Southeast Asian cooking. It is widely available and can easily be grown at home. **Coriander leaves** are used as a herb and a garnish. They are sold in bunches, sometimes with the roots still attached. Small, round **coriander seeds** have a mild citrus fragrance. The seeds are used whole, or ground into a powder that is the basis for many curries and sauces.

Cumin seeds (*jintan putih*) are pale brown to black in colour and ridged on the outside. They impart an earthy flavour and are used whole, or roasted and then ground to a fine powder. Cumin seeds are usually partnered with coriander seeds in basic spice mixtures, and are often dry-roasted or fried in oil to intensify their flavour.

Curry leaves are the tiny, slender leaves of the curry leaf shrub that belongs to the same family as the lemon tree. They do not taste like curry but are so-named because of their frequent use in Indian curries. They are sold in sprigs of 12–16 small, slightly pointed, green leaves with a distinct fragrance often associated with Indian curries. Do not substitute with Indonesian *daun salam* or bay leaves as sometimes suggested, as the flavour is totally different. There is no substitute for curry leaves.

Curry powder is a commercial spice blend that generally includes cumin seeds, coriander seeds, turmeric, ginger, cinnamon and cloves. Different spice combinations vary in colour and flavour. They are sold for various types of curries—meat, fish or chicken. Use an all-purpose blend if a specific curry powder is not available.

are available and must be soaked in hot water for 20–30 minutes before use. A better substitute is water-packed jars of sliced galangal exported from Thailand, where it is called *kha*. Try to get fresh galangal root whenever possible.

Daikon radishes are large root vegetables also known as white radishes or giant radishes. They are juicy and bland in flavour. They can grow to a length of 40 cm (15 in) or more. Choose firm and heavy daikons without any bruises on them. Scrub or peel the skin before you grate or slice the flesh.

Fennel seeds have an appearance very similar to cumin seeds, but are larger and paler. They add a sweet fragrance to a number of Malay and Indian dishes, with a flavour similar to liqourice or anise. The seeds are used whole or ground. They are sometimes mistakenly called anise in Malaysia.

Garlic chives or Chinese chives have flat leaves about 30 cm (12 in) long. They are used both as a vegetable and a seasoning. They have a more emphatic, garlicky flavour than Western chives and resemble flat spring onions.

Dried black Chinese mushrooms should be soaked in warm water for 20 minutes before use, and the tough stems discarded. These mushrooms vary in thickness and quality. Try to buy the thickest ones for dishes that feature mushrooms as the main ingredient.

Fenugreek seeds are flat and slightly rectangular, about 3 mm (⅛ in) long, light brown in colour, with a deep furrow along their lengths. They are bitter, so use sparingly.

Ghee is rich clarified butter oil with all the milk solids removed. Widely used in Indian cooking, it can be heated to high temperatures without burning, and adds a rich and delicious flavour to foods, although it is very high in cholesterol. Available canned in supermarkets and Indian provision shops. Substitute butter or vegetable oil.

Fermented soybean paste (*tau cheo*) contains soft, slightly fermented soybeans in a salty brown sauce that has a distinctive tang. They are lightly mashed and used to season fish, noodle and some vegetable dishes. Sold in jars in the supermarket, the basic fermented soybean paste contains only soybeans, water and salt. Sweetened versions, or those with added chilli and garlic, are also available. Miso is a good substitute.

Hoisin sauce or Peking sauce is a sweet and spicy reddish-brown sauce made from soybeans, garlic, pepper and various spices. It is commonly used as a dipping sauce for pork and duck dishes, and as a flavouring in stews. The bottled sauce keeps indefinitely if stored in the refrigerator.

Dried prawns are a popular Asian ingredient, particularly for sauces and sambals. They are tiny, orange-coloured saltwater prawns that have been dried in the sun. They come in different sizes and the really small ones have their heads and tails still attached. Look for prawns that are pink and plump, avoiding any with a grayish appearance. The better quality ones are bright orange in colour and shelled. Dried prawns will keep for several months. They should be soaked in warm water for 5 minutes to soften slightly before use.

Galangal (*lengkuas*) is a very fragrant root belonging to the ginger family. It imparts a distinctive flavour to many dishes. Try to find young, pinkish galangal as it is more tender. Always peel and slice the root before grinding as it is tough. Slices of dried galangal

Ikan bilis or baby anchovies are tiny whitebait fish ranging from 2–5 cm (1–2 in) in length. They are usually sold in Asia salted and sun-dried. Remove the head and black intestinal tract before using. If possible, buy them split, cleaned and ready for use. *Ikan bilis* are usually quite salty, so taste any dish using *ikan bilis* before adding more salt. They are used as a seasoning or deep-fried with chillies and peanuts to make a crunchy side dish or appetiser (Chilli Peanuts with Anchovies, page 33).

Kaffir lime leaves (*daun limau purut*) add an intense fragrance to soups and curries of Malay or Nonya origin. The leaves are added whole to curries, or finely shredded and added to salads, giving a wonderfully tangy taste. They are commonly used in Indonesian and Thai cooking, and are available frozen or dried in supermarkets. Frozen leaves are more flavourful than the dried ones.

Kangkung is a highly nutritious vegetable also known as water spinach.

Young shoots are served as part of a mixed platter of raw vegetables for dipping in hot sauces, while the leaves and tender tips are often stir-fried. Substitute *bok choy* or spinach.

Keropok are dried wafers made from tapioca starch mixed with bits of prawn or fish, which are deep-fried until crispy then eaten as a garnish or snack. The wafers must be thoroughly dried before deep-frying in oil for a few seconds, when they puff up spectacularly. Store fried *keropok* in an airtight container.

Laksa leaves (*daun kesum*) known in English as polygonum, is a fragrant herb that is traditionally added to *laksa* stews (pages 75, 76). The spear-shaped leaves wilt quickly once they are plucked off the stem and have an intense fragrance reminiscent of lemon with a hint of eucalyptus. Substitute mint and coriander leaves.

Lemongrass is a fragrant lemony stalk used whole in soups and curries, or ground as part of a basic spice mix. Lemongrass stems are usually sold in bunches of 3–4 stems in the supermarket. The tough outer layers should be peeled away and only the thick lower third of the stem is used. Always slice the stems crosswise before grinding to get a smooth paste.

Limes of two varieties are used in Malaysia. The larger limes, *limau nipis*, are slightly smaller than average Western limes, and change from green to yellow when ripe. The smaller *limau kasturi* or kalamansi limes are slightly less acidic and more fragrant. The grated rind is also used in cooking.

Fresh yellow wheat noodles (*mee*)

Fresh flat rice noodles (*kway teow*)

Fresh *laksa* rice noodles

Dried rice vermicelli (*beehoon*)

Dried mung bean glass noodles (*tanghoon*)

Noodles are a universal favourite in Malaysia which the Malays, Nonyas and Indians have enthusiastically adopted from the Chinese. Both fresh and dried noodles made from either wheat, rice or mung bean flour are found. **Fresh yellow wheat noodles** (Hokkien *mee*) are heavy, spaghetti-like noodles made from wheat flour and egg. They are also used for Malay Mee Rebus and Indian Mee Goreng. **Fresh flat rice noodles** (*kway teow*) are ribbon-like noodles about 1 cm (½ in) wide are used in soups or fried. **Fresh *laksa* rice noodles** look like white spaghetti and are made from rice flour and traditionally used in *laksa* dishes. **Dried rice vermicelli** (*beehoon*) are very fine rice threads that must be plunged into boiling water to soften before use. **Dried mung bean glass noodles** (*tanghoon*) with fine white strands are generally used in soups. They are also called "cellophane" or "transparent" noodles, all accurate descriptions of their appearance after soaking. Both fresh and dried noodles need to be blanched in boiling water before cooking—use a pair of long chopsticks to keep the noodles from sticking together while they are cooking.

Mint leaves are sold as fresh sprigs or dried and minced. Store fresh mint in the refrigerator, wrapped in paper towels and sealed in a plastic bag. Bottles of dried mint leaves should be stored away from light, heat and moisture. Just before use, crush the dried leaves in your palm to release their flavour.

Mustard seeds (*biji sawi*) are small, round and either brownish black or yellow in colour. Brown-black mustard seeds are used in southern Indian cuisines and impart a nutty flavour to dishes. Do not substitute with yellow mustard seeds as the flavour is different.

Okra, known locally as ladies' fingers, is usually partnered with eggplants in Indian fish curries. The vegetable has green, curved ridges and ranges from 7–20 cm (3–8 in) in length. They contain edible white seeds and a sticky juice used for thickening some dishes.

Oyster sauce is the rich, thick and dark extract of dried oysters. It is frequently added to stir-fried vegetable and meat dishes, and must be refrigerated once the bottle is opened. Expensive versions made with abalone and vegetarian versions made from mushrooms are also available. Choose carefully as most brands are loaded with MSG.

Palm sugar (*gula melaka*) is made from the sap of coconut or *arenga* palms. It comes in rectangular or cylindrical blocks and varies in colour from gold to light brown with a strong caramel taste. Substitute dark brown sugar or maple syrup.

Pandanus leaves impart a subtle fragrance and colour to a range of Malay and Nonya dishes. They are usually tied in a knot and then boiled. Bottled pandanus extract can be substituted in desserts, but if fresh or dried pandanus leaves are not available, omit them altogether from savoury dishes.

Rice flour is made from ground uncooked rice grains. It is used to make doughs and batters for many desserts. Fresh rice flour was traditionally made by soaking rice overnight and then slowly grinding it in a stone mill. The same result may be achieved by grinding soaked rice in a blender. It is sold in packets in supermarkets and Asian provision shops.

Rice wine is added to marinades and stir-fried dishes in much the same way that sherry is used in Western cooking. Substitute sake or dry sherry.

Sago pearls are dried beads of sago starch obtained by grinding the pith of the sago palm tree to a paste and then pressing it through a sieve. The pearls are glutinous, with little taste and are used in Asian desserts. Sago pearls must be rinsed in water and drained to remove excess starch before use. They are sold in various sizes and colours. Available in plastic packets in grocery stores.

Salted fish is used in Malaysian cooking as a seasoning or condiment. It should be soaked in water before use to remove some of the salt. Slice and fry the fish until crisp to use as a side dish or appetiser.

Sesame oil is extracted from roasted (darker oil) or raw (lighter oil) sesame seeds. It is used as a seasoning and never for stir-fries as high heat turns it bitter.

Spring onions are also known as scallions, green onions or sometimes as shallots. Spring onions have slender stalks with dark green leaves and white bases. They are sprinkled generously on soups and as a garnish.

Star anise is an eight-pointed dried pod encasing shiny black seeds that have a strong aniseed flavour. The whole spice is usually used in cooking and discarded before serving. Whole star anise keeps for a year in an airtight container.

Light soy sauce   Black soy sauce   Sweet black sauce

Soy sauce is brewed from soybeans, water, wheat and salt. Regular soy sauce is saltier and used as a table dip and cooking seasoning. **Black soy sauce** is denser and less salty than regular light soy sauce and adds a smoky flavour to dishes. **Sweet black sauce** (*tim cheong*) is a thick, fragrant sauce used in many marinades and sauces.

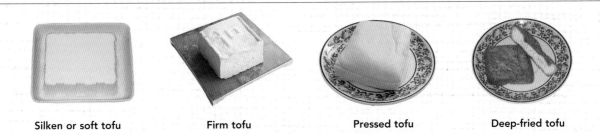

| Silken or soft tofu | Firm tofu | Pressed tofu | Deep-fried tofu |

Tofu is rich in protein and amazingly versatile. Various types of tofu, originally introduced by the Chinese, are now used by almost every ethnic group in Malaysia. **Silken** or **soft tofu** has a very fine texture, high water content and tends to break easily. **Firm tofu** holds its shape better when cut or cooked and has a stronger, slightly sour taste. **Pressed tofu** (often confusingly labelled as firm tofu) has much of the moisture extracted and is therefore much firmer in texture and excellent for stir-fries. Refrigerate fresh tofu immersed in water. Small cubes of **deep-fried tofu** (*tau foo pok*) are added to slow-cooked dishes and some soups.

Starfruit is a large five-edged fruit also known as carambola or *belimbing manis*. It has a distinct sweet and tart taste. Starfruit is usually thinly sliced and eaten raw.

Tamarind pulp (*asam*) is the fruit of the tamarind tree seed pod. It is sold dried in packets or jars and generally still has some seeds and pod fibres mixed in with the dried pulp. It is used as a souring agent in many Malaysian dishes. To obtain **tamarind juice**, soak the pulp in warm water for 5 minutes, mash well and then strain and discard any seeds and fibres. If using already cleaned tamarind pulp, slightly reduce the amounts called for in the recipes. The dried pulp keeps indefinitely in an airtight container.

Turmeric (*kunyit*) is a root similar to ginger in but with a bright yellow colour and a more pungent flavour. Turmeric has antiseptic and astringent qualities and stains everything permanently, so scrub your knife blade, hands and chopping board immediately after handling. Purchase fresh turmeric root as needed as the flavour fades after a few days. Substitute 1 teaspoon turmeric powder for 2½ cm (1 in) of the fresh root.

Turmeric leaves are the large leaves of the turmeric plant that are used in some parts of Asia for cooking. They can also be thinly sliced and eaten with Nasi Ulam (page 59) and are seldom available outside Asia.

Water chestnuts are roots about the size of chestnuts that are crunchy, white and juicy-sweet inside. The dark brown skins should be peeled before eating, and it is well worth the effort of using fresh water chestnuts if you can find them. Their crisp texture and sweet flavour make them popular in salads, stir-fried vegetable dishes and desserts. Store refrigerated, immersed in water, for up to a week.

White vinegar called for in the recipes in this book is the normal distilled vinegar sold in bottles in supermarkets. Some Malaysian cooks prefer rice vinegar or cider vinegar instead, and Chinese chefs often prefer black vinegar. Vinegar is used to make condiments or as a preservative and any type of vinegar may be substituted. When cooking with vinegar, use unreactive utensils made of stainless steel, glass, enamel or some hardy plastics.

Wild ginger buds (*bunga kantan*) are the pink buds of wild ginger plants, also known as torch ginger. They are highly aromatic and lend a subtle but distinct fragrance to dishes of Malay and Nonya origin. Ginger buds are available in fresh markets and supermarkets.

Wonton wrappers are square or round wrappers made of flour, eggs and water. The thin ones are used for dumplings in soups while the thicker ones are used for frying. Sold in the refrigerated or freezer sections of supermarkets, or make your own fresh ones (page 46). Frozen wrappers should be thawed to room temperature before use.

AUTHENTIC MALAYSIAN RECIPES

Portions

In homes and restaurants throughout Malaysia and most of Asia, food is seldom served in individual portions. Main dishes and condiments are normally placed on the table for people to help themselves, family style. Small amounts of these dishes are eaten with copious quantities of fragrant, fluffy rice, sticky glutinous rice or wheat or rice noodles. This makes it difficult to estimate the exact number of portions each recipe will provide. As a general rule, however, the recipes in this book will serve 4–6 people as part of a meal with rice and three other main dishes.

Malaysian Seasonings

Malaysians are fond of strong flavours—spicy, salty, sour and sweet. The amounts of chilli, soy sauce, sugar and lime juice given in the following recipes are guides, not absolute measures. Bear in mind that you can always increase the amount of seasonings later when preparing a dish. Seasonings may also be added individually at the table, so be careful not to overdo it in the initial stages.

Sambals, Dips And Achars

The recipes on pages 33–35 for sauces and condiments can be prepared in larger quantities and stored in a refrigerator or freezer for some time afterward. No Malaysian home is complete without a small bottle of one of these sambals or pickles in the refrigerator.

Time Estimates

Estimates are given for food preparation and cooking, and are based on the assumption that a food processor or blender will be used to grind spices.

Ingredients

Many Malaysian ingredients are now available in well-stocked supermarkets outside Malaysia—including coriander leaf (cilantro), galangal root, coconut cream, palm sugar and lemongrass. If you're not in Malaysia or a neighbouring region, look for ingredients that are more difficult to find in Asian specialty shops. Items like *belachan* (dried prawn paste) and black soy sauce or wild ginger buds are essential in the preparation of certain dishes. Check the ingredient listings on pages 26–31 for alternate names. You can also check the Internet listings on page 111 for possible sources. If still difficult to locate, see pages 26–31 for possible substitutes.

Tips on Grinding Spices

When using a mortar and pestle or blender to prepare spice pastes, it helps to peel and slice the ingredients finely before grinding. Grind tougher ingredients first before grinding the softer ones. Add a little liquid (oil, coconut milk or water, depending on the recipe) to keep the blades turning. Be sure not to overload the blender—if the quantity is too large, pulse them in batches and grind each batch before grinding the next. If you have to roast some ingredients before grinding, allow them to cool down before grinding. Spice pastes need only be ground coarsely—not to a purée. Store unused spice pastes in plastic wrap or an airtight container in the refrigerator or freezer.

MANGO CHUTNEY

Makes 1 cup
Preparation time: 15 mins
Cooking time: 30 mins

2 tablespoons oil
2 small unripe mangoes (300 g/
    10 oz total), peeled and cut into
    1 cm (½ in) cubes to yield 1 cup

SPICE PASTE
½ teaspoon cumin seeds
½ teaspoon fennel seeds
½ teaspoon coriander seeds
¼ teaspoon turmeric powder
1 cm (½ in) ginger, sliced
2 red chillies, deseeded and sliced
3 shallots, sliced
2 cloves garlic, sliced

WHOLE SPICES
2 cloves
½ cinnamon stick (2½ cm/1 in)
1 star anise pod
1 cardamom pod, lightly bruised

DRESSING
¼ cup (125 ml) white vinegar
1 heaped tablespoon raisins
3 tablespoons sugar
½ teaspoon salt

1. Grind the Spice Paste ingredients in a mortar or blender, adding a little oil if necessary to keep the blades turning.
2. Heat the remaining oil in a pan and stir-fry the Spice Paste and Whole Spices over medium heat until fragrant, about 10 minutes.
3. Add the Dressing ingredients and the mangoes to the pan. Reduce the heat to low and cook for 20 minutes until the mangoes are soft. Add 1½–2 tablespoons additional sugar if the mangoes are very sour. Store the chutney in the refrigerator for up to a month in a sealed jar. Serve as an accompaniment to meat and fish dishes.

MANGO KERABU

Makes 2 cups
Preparation time: 5 mins

Basic Chilli Sauce (page 35)
1 small ripe mango (about 250 g/
    8 oz), peeled and diced
4 mint leaves, coarsely chopped
4 coriander leaves (cilantro),
    coarsely chopped

Prepare the Basic Chilli Sauce. Add the mango, mint and coriander leaves, and mix well. Serve immediately as a side dish with rice meals.

CHILLI PEANUTS WITH ANCHOVIES

Makes 1¼ cups
Preparation time: 10 mins
Cooking time: 5 mins

4 red chillies, deseeded and sliced
1 shallot, peeled and halved
1 tablespoon oil
1 tablespoon sugar
½ teaspoon salt
¾ cup (100 g) roasted peanuts with
    skins intact
⅔ cup (30 g) *ikan bilis* (dried anchovies), heads and intestinal tracts removed and fried until crisp

Grind the chillies and shallot to a paste in a mortar or blender. Heat the oil and gently stir-fry the paste with the sugar and salt for 1 minute. Add the peanuts and *ikan bilis*, and stir-fry for another 3 minutes. Remove from the heat and set aside to cool. Keeps in the refrigerator for 3 weeks. Serve with *nasi lemak* for breakfast or as a snack or appetiser.

FRIED SHALLOTS

Makes ½ cup
Preparation time: 30 mins
Cooking time: 10 mins

125 g (4 oz) shallots
1 cup (250 ml) oil

1. Soak the shallots in salted water for 5 minutes, then peel and slice thinly. Pat dry the sliced shallots thoroughly with a paper towel.
2. Heat the oil in a skillet and stir-fry the shallots over moderate heat until golden brown and crispy. Drain and set aside to cool. Store in an airtight container for 2 to 3 weeks. Use as a crispy garnish on noodles, rice and vegetable dishes.

SAMBAL BELACHAN

Makes 1 cup
Preparation time: 15 mins

12 large red chillies, deseeded and
    sliced
2 tablespoons *belachan* (dried
    prawn paste), roasted
⅔ cup (165 ml) water
¼ cup (60 ml) lime juice

Blend the chillies and *belachan* with the water until coarse. Season with the lime juice. Keeps for 3 weeks in the refrigerator. Serve with rice, noodles and as a dip for fried foods.

STUFFED CHILLI PICKLE

Makes 2½ cups
Preparation time: 30 mins
Cooking time: 10 mins

1 small unripe papaya or 1 small white radish (about 600 g/20 oz)
1 tablespoon salt
4 green beans, sliced lengthwise halfway down
8 cm (3 in) piece cucumber, halved crosswise and cut into chunks
⅓ cup (50 g) cauliflower florets, broken into small pieces
½ cup (50 g) coarsely cut cabbage
8 shallots, pricked with a fork
2½ cm (1 in) ginger, thinly sliced
5 cloves garlic, slivered
1 teaspoon brown mustard seeds
2 heaped tablespoons dried prawns, soaked in warm water to soften
15 cm (6 in) fresh turmeric root or ¼ cup turmeric powder
2 teaspoons *belachan* (dried prawn paste)
2 tablespoons oil
1 cup (250 ml) white vinegar
5 tablespoons sugar
½ teaspoon salt
8 green chillies, straight, with stalks

1. Shred the papaya as thinly as possible. Sprinkle 1 teaspoon of the salt and set aside for 5 minutes. Then pat dry with paper towels. Spread the papaya strips evenly on a tray and bake in a preheated oven at 100°C (200°F) for 45 minutes to 1 hour, leaving the oven door slightly open. Toss the slices twice during baking. Alternatively, finely shred the white radish, sprinkle salt and set aside to dry for ½ day in the sun.
2. When the papaya or radish shreds are almost dry, prepare the beans, cucumber, cauliflower, cabbage and shallots. Sprinkle 1 teaspoon salt on the prepared vegetables and leave them in the sun for 2 to 3 hours. Alternatively, bake in a preheated oven at 100°C (200°F) for 1 hour with the oven door slightly open. Lightly salt the ginger and garlic, and sun dry separately for 2 to 3 hours.
3. Grind the mustard seeds, dried prawns, turmeric, salted garlic and *belachan* in a mortar or blender, adding a little of the oil if necessary to keep the blades turning. Heat the oil in a small pot over medium heat and stir-fry the ground ingredients until fragrant, about 7 minutes. Add the vinegar, sugar and salt, and stir until dissolved. Remove from the heat and set aside.
4. Slit each chilli lengthwise, leaving about ½ cm (¼ in) at both ends intact. Use a sharp knife to gently remove the seeds and the membrane inside the chillies, then stuff each chilli

BASIC CHILLI SAUCE

Makes ½ cup (125 ml)
Preparation time: 5 mins
Cooking time: 2 mins

4 red chillies, deseeded and sliced
3 tablespoons water
2 tablespoons white vinegar
1 tablespoon sugar
½ teaspoon salt

Blend the chillies and water in a mortar or blender. Add the blended mixture and the rest of the ingredients to a pan and bring to a boil. Then remove from the heat and set aside to cool. Serve with fried rice, noodles, fritters and deep-fried foods. Keeps refrigerated for 3 months.

CUCUMBER AND PINEAPPLE ACHAR

Makes 2 cups
Preparation time: 15 mins

1 small cucumber (about 200 g/ 7 oz), peeled, deseeded and diced
¼ pineapple (150 g/5 oz), peeled and diced
1 red chilli, thinly sliced
1 small onion, sliced
2 tablespoons lime juice
1 tablespoon sugar
¼ teaspoon salt

Combine all the ingredients in a small salad bowl. Keeps refrigerated for 3 days. Serve as a condiment with spicy rice and chicken.

PICKLED PAPAYA

Makes 1¾ cups
Preparation time: 20 mins
Cooking time: 5 mins

½ small almost-ripe papaya (about 300 g/10 oz)
¼ cup (60 ml) white vinegar
1½ tablespoons sugar
¼ teaspoon salt
3 *chili padi* (bird's-eye chillies), whole

1. Peel the papaya, halve lengthwise and deseed, then slice into very thin strips. Rinse the papaya strips and pat dry.
2. Bring the vinegar, sugar and salt to a boil in a small saucepan. Remove from the heat and allow to cool.
3. Add the chillies and papaya strips, and transfer to a covered container. Keeps in the refrigerator for a month.

CHILLI GINGER SAUCE

Makes ¾ cup (180 ml)
Preparation time: 10 mins

4 red chillies, sliced
3 cm (1¼ in) ginger, sliced
3 cloves garlic
5 tablespoons water
1½ tablespoons sugar
1½ tablespoons lime juice
1 teaspoon salt
½ teaspoon sesame oil

Grind the chillies, ginger, garlic with water in a mortar or blender. Season with the sugar, lime juice, salt and sesame oil. Keeps in the refrigerator for 1 week. Serve with chicken rice.

with the dried papaya or radish. Mix with the prepared vegetables and ginger.
5. Pack the chillies and vegetables into jars. Pour the vinegar mixture over and seal each jar well. Set the jars aside for 3 days before serving the pickle. Keeps for at least 1 month without refrigeration. Serve with rice-based meals as a side dish.

CHICKEN CURRY PUFF

A perennial favourite originally created by Indian cooks and enjoyed by every Malaysian as a between-meal snack. You can find hot, fresh curry puffs sold by vendors at all hours of the day—even very early in the morning or very late at night. Spice up the puffs with chillies and chase them down with hot sweet milk tea—just like in Malaysia.

Makes 40 pieces
Preparation time: 45 mins + 45
  mins wrapping
Cooking time: 30 mins

FILLING
5 tablespoons oil
1 medium onion, diced
1 tablespoon grated ginger
3¹/₂ teaspoons meat curry powder
¹/₂ teaspoon chilli powder
¹/₂ teaspoon turmeric powder
2 large potatoes (500 g/1 lb total),
  peeled, boiled and diced
2 teaspoons sugar
¹/₂ teaspoon freshly ground black
  pepper
1 teaspoon salt
2 cups chicken meat (400 g/14 oz) or
  2 large chicken breasts, cooked
  and diced
¹/₄ cup (60 ml) water

PASTRY
3¹/₃ cups (500 g) flour
150 g (5 oz) butter or margarine
³/₄ cup + 4 teaspoons (200 ml) water
¹/₂ teaspoon salt

1. Heat the oil in a skillet over medium heat and gently stir-fry the onion and ginger until the onion turns light golden brown. Add the curry, chilli and turmeric powders, and stir-fry for 3 minutes or until fragrant. Add the potatoes, sugar, pepper and salt, and stir-fry for another 10 minutes. Then, add the chicken and water, and cook for 7 minutes, or until the mixture is almost dry. Remove from the heat and set aside to cool.
2. Knead the Pastry ingredients into a smooth dough. Cover with a damp cloth and set aside to rest in a warm place for 30 minutes to 1 hour.
3. Divide the dough into 2 portions. Roll each half on a lightly floured surface to 3 mm (¹/₈ in) thick. Use a curry puff cutter or a cookie cutter, to cut the dough into circles 10 cm (4 in) in diameter. Spoon 1 tablespoon of the Filling onto the centre of each circle. Fold the dough over to form a crescent and crimp and roll the edges to form a simple wave pattern, sealing the package well. Repeat until all the Filling and dough are used up.
4. Deep-fry each puff in hot oil until light golden brown on both sides. Alternately, bake at 180°C (350°F) for 30 minutes until light golden brown. Serve hot or at room temperature.

NOTE: Not all types of margarine are suitable to make the Pastry because of their high moisture content. The Malaysian brand, Planta, is recommended while Crisco is a suitable substitute. For variety in taste and colour, combine 1 boiled potato with fresh peas and a small carrot to make 750 g (1¹/₄ lbs) for the Filling, or combine 300 g (10 oz) boiled potato mixed with 5 hard-boiled eggs cut into cubes.

NONYA 'TOP HATS' Kuih Pie Tee

Delightfully crispy little rimmed cases with a colourful vegetable filling are a much-loved Nonya teatime treat.

Makes 30 Top Hats
Preparation time: 40 mins
Cooking time: 1 hour 10 mins

1 egg, fried into an omelette and thinly sliced, to garnish
Spring onion, thinly sliced, to garnish
Red chilli, thinly sliced, to garnish
Basic Chilli Sauce (page 35), to serve

CASES
2/3 cup (100 g) flour
1/2 teaspoon rice flour
1 egg, beaten
3/4 cup (175 ml) water
Pinch of salt
Oil for deep-frying
1 *kuih pie tee* mould (see photograph)

FILLING
1 tablespoon oil
3 cloves garlic, minced
150 g (5 oz) medium fresh prawns, peeled, deveined and diced
1 small *bangkuang* (jicama) (about 500 g/1 lb), sliced into thin shreds to yield 4 cups
1 large carrot (about 200 g), sliced into thin shreds
1 teaspoon freshly ground black pepper
1 teaspoon salt
1 teaspoon sugar

NOTE: It is essential that the oil and the mould is at the right temperature when cooking. It may take a few tries to successfully create "top hat" cases with rims. If not, simply make straight-sided ones. The mould is available in shops selling utensils and ingredients from Malaysia and Singapore.

---

1. Prepare the Basic Chilli Sauce by following the instructions on page 35.
2. To make the Cases, sift both the flours together into a mixing bowl, add the egg, water and salt, and mix well to form a smooth batter. Strain the batter to remove any lumps.
3. Heat the oil in a wok over medium heat until very hot. Dip the mould into the oil briefly, then remove and dip (leaving 1/8 from the top exposed) into the batter to coat it well. The batter should not sizzle when the mould is dipped into it. Lift the mould out of the batter and allow the excess batter to drip off. Then quickly plunge the mould into the hot oil and gently jiggle it up-and-down. The batter will slowly open and slip away from the mould. Cook the batter until light golden brown, then remove from the oil, drain and set aside to cool. Repeat until all the batter is used up. Store the Cases in an airtight container to keep them crispy.
4. To make the Filling, heat the oil in a wok or skillet over medium heat and stir-fry the garlic and prawns until lightly browned. Add the *bangkuang*, carrot, pepper, salt and sugar. Stir-fry for 5 minutes until the vegetables are tender.
5. To assemble, place a little Filling in each Case and top with a little of each garnish. Serve with a small bowl of Basic Chilli Sauce on the side.

ROTI CANAI Flaky Fried Indian Bread

A really good Roti Canai is feather-light, crispy, non-greasy and some would say, the Indian community's greatest culinary contribution to Malaysia. Roti Canai is a much lighter, flakier version of Roti Prata, another much loved Indian bread.

Makes 12 *roti*
Preparation time: 15 mins
Cooking time: 1 hour

1 tablespoon sweetened condensed milk or 2 tablespoons evaporated milk mixed with 1 tablespoon sugar
1½ cups (375 ml) water
5 cups (750 g) flour
2 eggs, beaten
1 teaspoon salt
2 tablespoons sugar
1 cup (250 ml) ghee or melted butter

1. Mix the sweetened condensed milk or evaporated milk mixture with the water and set aside.
2. Sift the flour into a mixing bowl. Add the eggs, salt, sugar and 5 tablespoons of ghee or melted butter, and mix well. Add the diluted sweetened condensed milk or evaporated milk mixture and knead for 10 minutes to make a soft dough. Shape the dough into a ball and place it in a small bowl. Cover with a damp cloth and set aside in a warm place to rest for 30 minutes.
3. Portion the dough into 12 pieces and roll each piece into a small ball. Coat each dough ball in the ghee or oil, cover and set aside again for at least 20 minutes or up to 4 hours.
4. Heat an iron griddle or heavy pan and grease with a little ghee or butter. Grease a rolling pin and work surface with ghee. Roll out each dough ball to make it as thin as possible. Then fold the edges inward to form a circular dough about 15 cm (6 in) in diameter, and repeat—rolling and folding—about 5 times. This process gives the bread a layered texture. Repeat with all the dough balls.
5. Fry each dough individually on the hot griddle over medium to high heat until crisp and golden brown, about 3 minutes on each side, adding more of the ghee or oil as necessary. Best served hot with a spicy meat or fish curry.

> **NOTE:** It takes much skill to swing out the dough in circles to stretch it paper thin, as the "Roti Man" does with a theatrical flourish. A greased rolling pin and work surface will give you similarly delicious result.

POPIAH Fresh Spring Rolls

This Nonya version of a popular Chinese snack uses fresh ready-to-eat wrappers and is substantial enough for an entire meal.

Makes 12 Popiah
Preparation time: 1 hour 10 mins +
   10 mins assembling time
Cooking time: 35 mins

4 tablespoons oil
3 eggs, lightly beaten
20 large fresh popiah wrappers
20 long lettuce leaves
Sweet black sauce (*tim cheong*), to
   taste
10 cloves garlic, ground to a paste
6 red chillies, deseeded and sliced,
   then ground to a paste
1 cup (50 g) bean sprouts, blanched
   and drained well
⅓ cup (60 g) coarsely ground roasted
   peanuts
3 tablespoons Fried Shallots (page 33)

FILLING
8 shallots, halved
8 cloves garlic, halved
2 tablespoons fermented soybean
   paste (*tau cheo*)
1 *bangkuang* (jicama) (about 500 g/
   1 lb), peeled and sliced into thin
   shreds to yield 4 cups
1 cake deep-fried tofu (250 g/8 oz),
   thinly sliced or 1 cake firm tofu
   (250 g/8 oz), deep-fried and thinly
   sliced to yield 1½ cups
1 teaspoon black soy sauce
1½ tablespoons sugar
½ teaspoon salt
125 g (4 oz) small fresh prawns, peeled
   and deveined
¼ small cabbage, thinly sliced into
   shreds to yield 2 cups
1 cup (125 g) green beans, thinly sliced

NOTE: Popiah wrappers are
similar to fresh Filipino wrappers,
lumpia. They are available in the
refrigerator or freezer sections in
Asian supermarkets.

---

1. Grease an omelette pan with ½ teaspoon of the oil and fry the eggs to make 3 very thin omelettes. Slice the omelettes into shreds and set aside.

2. To make the Filling, grind the shallots and garlic, and mix with the fermented soybean paste. Heat the rest of the oil in a pan over medium heat and stir-fry the paste mixture until fragrant, about 3 minutes. Spoon 1 table-spoon of the fried paste into a small bowl and set aside. Add the *bangkuang* to the remaining fried paste in the pan and cook for 5 minutes until soft. Then add the tofu and cook over low heat for 15 to 20 minutes. Season with the soy sauce, sugar and salt. Remove from the heat and set aside.

3. Place 1 teaspoon of the re-served paste in a wok with the prawns. Stir-fry for 3 minutes until the prawns are cooked and place in a small bowl. Repeat with the cabbage and beans, and place the cooked ingredients in another 2 bowls.

4. To serve, place the prepared ingredients on a table. Lay a popiah wrapper on a plate and place a lettuce leaf on it. Spread a little sweet black sauce, garlic paste and chilli paste on the leaf. Add a portion of the *bangkuang*, prawns, cabbage, beans, bean sprouts, peanuts and Fried Shallots. Fold in the sides of the popiah wrapper, roll and serve immediately.

BORNEO FISH CEVICHE

Fresh fish marinated in lemon juice and spiced with lashings of ginger, shallots and chillies is a favourite among Sarawak's Melanau people, who call their version Umai, while the Kadazans of Sabah call it Hinava.

Serves 4–6
Preparation time: 20 mins

500 g (1 lb) fresh white fish
   (Spanish mackerel preferred)
⅓ cup (85 ml) freshly squeezed lime
   or lemon juice
2–3 red chillies, sliced
1 teaspoon salt
6–8 shallots, thinly sliced
5 cm (2 in) ginger, slivered
2 sprigs fresh coriander leaves
   (cilantro), coarsely chopped
2 sprigs Chinese celery or Italian
   parsley, coarsely chopped

1. Remove all the skin and bones from the fish. Then cut the flesh into thin slices. Reserve 2 tablespoons of lime juice and marinate the fish in the rest of the juice for at least 30 minutes, stirring once or twice, until the fish turns white. Drain the fish and discard the lime juice.
2. While the fish is marinating, grind the chillies and salt until fine. When the fish is ready, mix it with the ground chillies, shallots, ginger, fresh herbs and reserved lime juice. Season with more salt if desired. Serve immediately as an appetiser or as part of a rice-based meal.

STIR-FRIED GREENS WITH BELACHAN

Cekuk manis (*Sauropus albicans*), a shrub with edible leaves, grows wild throughout Southeast Asia. A vegetable grower in Lahad Datu, Sabah, discovered a method to make it grow quickly so that the stems are edible, earning it the name Sabah vegetable or Sabah asparagus. It has a flavour similar to *kangkung* (water spinach) which is a good substitute.

Serves 4
Preparation time: 15 mins
Cooking time: 10 mins

300 g (10 oz) *kangkung*, spinach or
   Sabah vegetable
2 red chillies, sliced
2 shallots, peeled and halved
1 clove garlic, peeled and bruised
½ teaspoon *belachan* (dried prawn
   paste)
1 tablespoon oil
½ teaspoon salt

1. Wash, drain and coarsely chop the *kangkung* or spinach. Alternatively, pinch off the tough stems on the Sabah vegetable and cut into 5 cm (2 in) lengths.
2. Grind the chillies, shallots, garlic and *belachan* to a coarse paste.
3. Heat the oil in a wok and stir-fry the ground mixture for 2 to 3 minutes or until fragrant. Add the vegetables and stir-fry briskly for another 5 minutes until the vegetables are wilted and just cooked. Season with salt and serve.

SUPERIOR WONTON SOUP

Juicy, stuffed dumplings or wonton in soup are found in Chinese restaurants throughout the world. This version is definitely a cut above the rest, with an excellent stock made from *ikan bilis*, dried scallops and chicken.

Makes 15 wonton
Preparation time: 40 mins
Cooking time: 1 hour 10 mins

1 cup (100 g) snow peas or 1½ cups (100 g) *bok choy*, blanched for a few seconds and sliced
6 dried black Chinese mushrooms, soaked, boiled and thinly sliced
Pepper to taste (optional)
Green chilli, sliced, to serve
Soy sauce, to serve
Chilli Ginger Sauce (page 35)

BASIC STOCK
300 g (10 oz) chicken bones or chicken meat
3 dried scallops
½ cup (90 g) very small dried *ikan bilis* (baby anchovies or whitebait)
5 stalks celery ribs, cut into lengths
3 cloves garlic, peeled and bruised
1 medium carrot, cut into chunks
1 cm (½ in) ginger, peeled and bruised
½ teaspoon white peppercorns
10 cups (2½ litres) water

WONTON WRAPPERS
1¾ cups (270 g) flour
½ cup (125 ml) water
1 egg

FILLING
200 g (7 oz) medium fresh prawns, peeled and deveined
150 g (5 oz) minced chicken or pork
8 water chestnuts, peeled and diced
50 g (1½ oz) dried black fungus, or 4 dried mushrooms, soaked in water for 15 minutes to soften
1 egg, beaten
2 teaspoons rice wine
2 teaspoons soy sauce
1 teaspoon oyster sauce
1 teaspoon grated ginger juice
½ teaspoon sesame oil
1 teaspoon cornstarch
1 teaspoon sugar
½ teaspoon salt
½ teaspoon ground white pepper

1. Prepare the Chilli Ginger Sauce by following the instructions on page 35.
2. Place the Basic Stock ingredients in a stockpot and bring to a boil. Skim the surface, lower the heat and simmer, covered, for 1 hour. Strain the stock well and discard the solids. Reserve 6 cups (1½ litres) of the stock.
3. Make the Wonton Wrappers by kneading the flour, water and egg for 10 minutes into a smooth dough. Set the dough aside to rest for 15 minutes. Pinch about 1 tablespoon of the dough and roll it into a small ball. Place the dough ball on a work surface and flatten it with your palm. Roll the dough out into a 3½ in (9 cm) circle and set aside on a dry plate. Repeat with the rest of the dough to make at least 15 wrappers in all.

4. To make the Filling, chop the prawns, chicken, water chestnuts and black fungus or mushrooms together with a cleaver until fine. Add all the other ingredients and mix well.
5. Place a wrapper on a lightly floured surface and scoop 1 teaspoon of the Filling onto the centre of a wrapper and dab a little water on the wrapper all around the Filling. Fold the wrapper up like a pouch and press the edges to seal it. Repeat until all the Filling is used up to make 15 wonton pouches.
6. Bring the reserved stock back to a boil, add the wonton and simmer for 3 to 5 minutes or until they rise to the top. Add the snow peas, mushrooms and pepper. Remove from the heat and serve immediately with small bowls of sliced green chillies in soy sauce and Chilli Ginger Sauce on the side.

NOTE: Wonton wrappers are available ready-made in the refrigerator or freezer sections of most supermarkets. If using frozen wrappers, allow them to thaw to room temperature before using. If you are unable to find dried scallops (which are very expensive), substitute 500 g (1 lb) of pork bones to make the stock.

NONYA PRAWN SALAD WITH SWEET AND SOUR DRESSING

Contrasting flavours and textures bring excitement to this combination of vegetables, prawns, herbs and crunchy *keropok* prawn crackers. It makes a delicious starter to any meal.

Serves 6
Preparation time: 30 mins

1 head soft-leaf lettuce, torn into shreds (optional)
1 small carrot, cut into matchsticks
125 g (4 oz) daikon radish, cut into matchsticks
1 medium cucumber, halved lengthwise, deseeded and thinly sliced
1 starfruit or green apple, halved lengthwise and thinly sliced
2 ripe tomatoes, cut into wedges
250 g (8 oz) medium fresh prawns, poached for 1 minute, then peeled and deveined
Fresh coriander leaves (cilantro), to garnish
Fried Shallots (page 33), to garnish
Keropok (deep-fried prawn crackers), to garnish (optional)
Fried peanuts, skins removed and coarsely ground, to garnish (optional)

SWEET SOUR DRESSING
7–10 red chillies, deseeded and sliced
3–4 cloves garlic, peeled and bruised
$\frac{1}{2}$ cup (125 ml) Chinese plum sauce or $\frac{1}{2}$ cup (125 ml) tamarind juice (from 2 heaped tablespoons tamarind pulp mashed with $\frac{1}{4}$ cup (60 ml) water and strained) mixed with 1 tablespoon sugar
$\frac{1}{2}$ cup (125 ml) Palm Sugar Syrup (see note)
$\frac{1}{2}$ cup (125 ml) freshly squeezed lime juice
1 tablespoon soy sauce
$\frac{1}{2}$ tablespoon sesame oil

1. To make the Sweet Sour Dressing, grind the chillies and garlic in a mortar or blender, adding a little of the plum sauce or tamarind juice to keep the blades turning. When finely ground, add the rest of the dressing ingredients and grind again. Set aside in a small bowl.
2. Prepare the rest of the ingredients and portion them onto 6 serving plates. Pour a little of the dressing over each serving and top with the fresh coriander leaves, crispy shallots, *keropok* and a generous helping of peanuts. Or serve the prepared ingredients with the dressing on the side.

NOTE: Different brands of Chinese plum sauce vary in their sugar content, so adjust the dressing to suit your taste. To prepare **Palm Sugar Syrup**, bring $\frac{1}{2}$ cup (100 g) palm sugar shavings and $\frac{1}{2}$ cup (125 ml) water to a boil. Add a pandanus leaf to the water, if desired. Then reduce the heat and simmer over low heat for 10 minutes or until the liquid thickens and becomes syrupy. Strain, discard the pandanus leaf if using, and set the syrup aside to chill. Some brands of palm sugar are very hard and need to be chopped with a sharp knife before boiling.

SPICY CURRIED PUMPKIN

Gourds are very popular among Malaysians of southern Indian origin, especially the sweet-tasting pumpkin that complements a mild mixture of curry spices used in this dish.

Serves 4
Preparation time: 25 mins
Cooking time: 20 mins

2 tablespoons oil
1 tablespoon brown mustard seeds
2 sprigs curry leaves
1 medium onion, diced
2 teaspoons chicken curry powder
1 teaspoon chilli powder
$\frac{1}{2}$ teaspoon turmeric powder
$\frac{1}{2}$ small pumpkin (about 500 g/1 lb), peeled and cut into chunks
$1\frac{1}{2}$ cups (375 ml) water
1 teaspoon salt

1. Heat the oil in a wok over high heat and stir-fry the mustard seeds and curry leaves for 2 minutes until the seeds pop. Add the onion and stir-fry gently for 3 minutes until the onion is light golden brown.
2. Add the curry, chilli and turmeric powders, and stir-fry for 30 seconds. Then add the pumpkin chunks and stir to coat them well with the spices. Slowly add the water, stirring constantly, and season with the salt. Simmer, uncovered, over medium heat until the pumpkin is tender and dry, about 15 to 20 minutes. Best served hot.

SNAKE GOURD AND LENTILS WITH MUSTARD SEEDS

Colours and textures contrast beautifully in this southern Indian dish. Snake gourd is very popular with Indian cooks throughout Southeast Asia and should be eaten when young. As the snake gourd has a bitter taste, it is often regarded as a tonic and is used in traditional medicine.

Serves 4
Preparation time: 15 mins
Cooking time: 25 mins

½ cup (100 g) dried yellow lentils, rinsed thoroughly
½ teaspoon turmeric powder
2 cups (500 ml) water
1 snake gourd, summer squash or zucchini (about 500 g/1 lb)
2 tablespoons oil
1 tablespoon brown mustard seeds
4 shallots, sliced
1 clove garlic, sliced
1 teaspoon salt
1 sprig curry leaves
2 red chillies, deseeded and sliced

1. Mix the lentils and turmeric powder in the water and simmer, uncovered, in a saucepan for 15 minutes or until the lentils are soft. Drain the lentils and set aside.
2. While the lentils are cooking, prepare the gourd. Halve the gourd lengthwise, discard the pulpy centre and cut crosswise into ½ cm (½ in) slices.
3. Heat the oil in a skillet and stir-fry the mustard seeds until they pop. Add the shallots and garlic, and stir-fry gently until soft. Add the boiled lentils, snake gourd and salt, and cook for another 5 to 7 minutes or until the gourd is tender. Add the curry leaves and chillies, and remove from the heat. Serve with rice.

NOTE: Snake gourd is a long, thin gourd with dark green skin and slightly bitter taste. Look for it in Indian shops. Dried yellow lentils are tiny discs available in packets in Indian shops.

PRAWN AND VEGETABLE SALAD

A family favourite during the Chinese New Year reunion dinner, when many other rich dishes are served.

Serves 4–6
Preparation time: 40 mins
Cooking time: 15 mins

2 tablespoons oil
2 cloves garlic, minced
200 g (7 oz) medium fresh prawns, peeled and diced
1/2 small dried squid (10 cm/4 in long), soaked in boiling water for 10 minutes
1 *bangkuang* (jicama) or daikon radish (about 500 g/1 lb), peeled and cut into matchsticks
1 medium carrot, peeled and cut into matchsticks
1/3 cup (85 ml) chicken stock or 1/4 teaspoon chicken stock granules mixed with 1/3 cup (85 ml) hot water (optional)
1/2 teaspoon white pepper
2 tablespoons soy sauce
Lettuce leaves, to serve
Hoisin sauce, to serve (optional)

1. Heat the oil in a wok and stir-fry the garlic until golden brown. Add the prawns and cook until they turn pink. Then add the squid and mix thoroughly. Add the *bangkuang* and carrot, and cook until the *bangkuang* starts to soften, about 7 minutes.
2. Add the chicken stock and simmer, stirring from time to time, until the vegetables are soft. Season with the pepper and soy sauce, and mix well. Serve the salad at room temperature on a bed of lettuce leaves. To eat, simply place the salad and a smear of hoisin sauce on a lettuce leaf and roll it up.

STIR-FRIED PEAS WITH PRAWNS AND GARLIC

Serves 4
Preparation time: 15 mins
Cooking time: 10 mins

1 teaspoon rice wine
1 tablespoon soy sauce
1 tablespoon oyster sauce
1 tablespoon oil
8 cloves garlic, unpeeled and lightly bruised
150 g (5 oz) medium fresh prawns, peeled and deveined
250 g (8 oz) sugar snap peas, blanched in boiling water for 5 seconds
1/4 cup (60 ml) water or chicken stock
1/2 teaspoon cornstarch blended in 2 teaspoons water
1/4 teaspoon salt
1/4 teaspoon sugar

1. Combine the rice wine, soy sauce and oyster sauce, and set aside.
2. Heat the oil in a wok until very hot and stir-fry the garlic for a few seconds. Add the prawns and stir-fry briskly until they change colour. Add the peas and oyster sauce mixture, and stir-fry for another 30 seconds, then add the water and bring to a boil. Thicken the broth with the cornstarch and season with salt and sugar. Serve immediately.

TROPICAL BANANA BUD SALAD WITH PRAWNS Pisang Jantung

No Malaysian with bananas growing in the garden would waste the bud of the banana flower, which is also sold in local markets and eaten like a vegetable. Surprisingly, it tastes very much like artichokes. This version of the very popular salad originates from the Portuguese community in Malacca.

Serves 4
Preparation time: 45 mins
Cooking time: 10 mins

1 fresh banana bud (about 250 g/8 oz)
  or ¼ cabbage (about 250 g/8 oz)
2 tablespoons oil
2 teaspoons dried prawns, soaked
  in warm water for 5 minutes to
  soften, drained and coarsely
  pounded or ground in a blender
⅓ cup (85 ml) thick coconut milk
¼ teaspoon salt
1 baby cucumber, sliced into matchsticks to yield 1 cup
6 small sour belimbing (baby starfruit) or 1 small unripe mango,
  thinly sliced into strips

1 fresh red chilli, deseeded and
  thinly sliced
4 shallots, sliced into rings
200 g (7 oz) medium fresh prawns,
  lightly poached for 1 minute, then
  peeled and deveined
Small limes (limau kasturi), halved,
  to serve

SPICE PASTE
3 red chillies, deseeded and sliced
6 shallots, peeled and halved
2 cloves garlic, peeled and halved
1 teaspoon belachan (dried prawn
  paste)
2 teaspoons sugar

1. Remove the outer red leaves of the banana bud and simmer the tender inner heart in lightly salted water for 20 minutes. Drain the bud and set aside to cool, then discard any hard parts in it. Halve the bud lengthwise, then cut crosswise into coarse slices. Set aside. If using cabbage, rinse, cut into thin slices and set aside.
2. Grind all the Spice Paste ingredients with 4 tablespoons of water to keep the blades turning.
3. Heat the oil in a skillet and gently stir-fry the dried prawns over moderate heat for half a minute. Then add the Spice Paste and stir-fry for another 2 to 3 minutes until fragrant. Add the coconut milk and salt, and stir. Remove from the heat and set aside to cool.
4. To serve, place the cooked banana bud or cabbage on the centre of a serving platter, top with the cucumber, belimbing or unripe mango slices, chilli, shallots and prawns. Drizzle the cooled sauce over the salad and toss lightly. Serve with the lime halves on the side.

> **NOTE:** If preferred, substitute 250 g (8 oz) shredded cooked chicken breast for the banana bud.

BEAN SPROUTS AND TOASTED COCONUT Taugeh Kerabu

This salad from the northern states of Peninsular Malaysia is an excellent accompaniment to rich or spicy dishes.

Serves 4
Preparation time: 15 mins
Cooking time: 10 mins

4 tablespoons fresh grated coconut
500 g (1 lb) bean sprouts
4 tablespoons oil
1/2 teaspoon sugar
1 1/2 teaspoons salt
1 red chilli, deseeded and sliced
   (optional)

SPICE PASTE
2 tablespoons dried prawns, rinsed
   and drained
5–6 red chillies, deseeded and sliced
4 shallots, peeled and halved
2 cloves garlic, peeled and halved

1. Dry-fry the grated coconut over low heat in a skillet, stirring constantly, until light golden brown, about 5 minutes. Set aside in a small plate or bowl to cool.
2. Blanch the bean sprouts in boiling water for a few seconds, then drain and plunge briefly into cold water. Set aside in a colander to drain.
3. Grind the Spice Paste ingredients to a paste in a mortar or blender. Heat the oil in a wok and stir-fry the paste over medium heat for 3 minutes until fragrant. Add the toasted coconut and bean sprouts, season with the sugar and salt, and stir-fry for a few seconds to mix well. Remove from the heat, garnish with the sliced chilli, if using, and serve immediately.

COCONUT SERUNDING

This dish is traditionally served as a topping.

Serves 8–10
Preparation time: 15 mins
Cooking time: 15 mins

1 coconut, freshly grated (about
   2 1/2 cups)
8 tablespoons oil
1 tablespoon fennel powder
2 slices *asam gelugur* or 1 teaspoon
   lime juice
1/2 teaspoon salt
1 teaspoon sugar
1 turmeric leaf, thinly sliced
   (optional)
4 kaffir lime leaves, thinly sliced

SPICE PASTE
2 stalks lemongrass, thick bottom
   third only, outer layers removed,
   inner part sliced
2 cm (3/4 in) fresh galangal root,
   sliced
1 cm (1/2 in) fresh turmeric root,
   sliced or 1 teaspoon turmeric
   powder

10–15 dried chillies, cut into lengths,
   soaked in warm water and
   deseeded
3 shallots, peeled and halved
3 cloves garlic, peeled and halved

1. Grind the Spice Paste ingredients in a mortar or blender, adding a little oil if necessary to keep the blades turning. Set aside.
2. Dry-fry the grated coconut in a skillet for about 5 minutes over low heat, stirring constantly until light golden brown. Set aside to cool in a small bowl.
3. Heat the oil in a skillet over medium heat and stir-fry the Spice Paste with the fennel powder and *asam gelugur* for 5 minutes (if using lime juice, do not add it in at this stage). Season with the salt,

sugar and lime juice, if using. Add the roasted coconut and continue to stir-fry over low heat until the coconut is crisp and dry, about 5 minutes. Add the turmeric leaf, if using, and kaffir lime leaves, and cook for another 3 minutes. Set aside to cool before serving.

NOTE: There are many variations to serunding—increase the amount of chillies used to make it more spicy or create an enticing flavour by seasoning with shredded cooked beef or coarsely ground deep-fried *ikan bilis*. Store serunding in a tightly sealed container for up to 3 weeks in the refrigerator.

RICE SALAD WITH FRESH HERBS

Nasi Ulam

A collection of wonderfully fragrant herbs normally found in a kitchen garden are combined with cooked rice to make this popular Kelantan dish. Any combination of common fresh herbs can be eaten with rice scented with lemongrass and lime leaves to make this very simple and absolutely delicious dish.

Serves 4–6
Preparation time: 30 mins
Cooking time: 20 mins

2 cups (400 g) uncooked rice, washed and drained
3 cups (750 ml) water
2 stalks lemongrass, thick bottom part only, outer layers removed, inner part bruised
2 cm (¾ in) galangal root, bruised
¼ teaspoon pandanus extract or 2 pandanus leaves, tied in a knot
2 kaffir lime leaves
2 tablespoons thick coconut milk
1 teaspoon salt

FRESH HERBS
3 daun salam (salam leaves) or 2 bunches coriander leaves (cilantro)
2 daun maduk or 2 sprigs fennel leaves
2 kaffir lime leaves or 2 sprigs chervil or parsley
2 sprigs daun selum or dill
2 sprigs laksa leaf or 1 sprig mint leaves
1 cekur (zedoary) leaf or 1 sprig spearmint
1 sprig Asian basil
1 turmeric leaf or 1 handful of lemon balm leaves
1 stalk daun renganga or 1 handful of chives
1 stalk lemongrass, thick bottom third only, outer layers removed, inner part only
1 shallot
1 wild ginger bud (bunga kantan) or 5 cm (2 in) fresh ginger
1 small cucumber, peeled and deseeded

1. Place the rice in a pan with the water, lemongrass, galangal, pandanus extract and lime leaves, coconut milk and salt. Bring to a boil, then reduce the heat to the minimum. Stir, cover and cook for 15 to 20 minutes until the rice is light and fluffy. Alternatively, cook in a rice cooker.
2. Slice all the Fresh Herbs very thinly and arrange in separate mounds on a large platter. Spoon the cooked rice onto the centre of the platter and allow each diner to help himself to the rice and herbs according to taste.

NOTE: In some Malaysian markets, bundles of mixed herbs are sold under the name ulam specially for use in this dish.

NASI KEMULI Spiced Nonya Wedding Rice

Simple but tasty, Nasi Kemuli is a must at Nonya weddings.

Serves 4
Preparation time: 10 mins
Cooking time: 40 mins

1 tablespoon ghee or oil
1½ cups (300 g) uncooked long-grain
    rice, washed and drained
1 teaspoon soy sauce
1 teaspoon salt
1 star anise pod
Raisins, to garnish

SPICE WATER
1 cup (60 g) coriander seeds
1 cinnamon stick (5 cm/2 in)
1 star anise pod
2 cloves
1 cardamom pod
5 cups (1¼ litres) water

SPICE PASTE
1 cm (½ in) ginger, sliced
3 shallots, peeled and halved
2 cloves garlic, peeled and halved
1 tablespoon fermented soybean
    paste (*tau cheo*)

1. Dry-fry the Spice Water dry ingredients in a skillet over medium heat for 1 minute. Then place them in a deep pan with the water and bring to a boil. Reduce the heat and simmer, uncovered, for 20 minutes until the liquid is reduced by half. Strain the Spice Water and set aside in a bowl. Discard the solids.
2. Grind the Spice Paste ingredients to a paste in a mortar or blender, adding a little oil if necessary to keep the blades turning.
3. Heat the ghee or oil in a pan over medium heat and gently stir-fry the Spice Paste for 2 to 3 minutes until fragrant. Remove from the heat, add the uncooked rice, soy sauce and salt, and mix well. Then add the star anise and reserved Spiced Water, stir, cover and cook over low heat until the liquid is absorbed and the rice is cooked, about 20 minutes. Garnish with the raisins and serve. Alternatively, place the fried Spice Paste and other ingredients in a rice cooker and turn it on.

CHILLI EGGPLANTS WITH BASIL Sambal Terong

This simple Nonya recipe using slender Asian eggplants includes fresh basil sprigs for added flavour.

Serves 4
Preparation time: 15 mins
Cooking time: 15 mins

2 small slender Asian eggplants
    (about 500 g/1 lb)
Oil for deep-frying
½ cup (10 g) Asian basil sprigs
½ teaspoon sugar

SPICE PASTE
3 red chillies, deseeded and sliced
1 teaspoon dried prawns, soaked
    in warm water to soften then
    drained
5 shallots, peeled and halved

4 cloves garlic, peeled and halved
1 tablespoon fermented soybean
    paste (*tau cheo*)

1. Grind the Spice Paste ingredients to a paste in a mortar or blender and set aside in a small bowl.
2. Wash the eggplants but do not peel them. Halve the eggplants length-wise, then halve them crosswise and pat dry.
3. Reserve 4 tablespoons of the oil and heat the rest of the oil in a wok. Deep-fry the eggplants in very hot oil for 3 minutes or until golden brown. Remove from the oil and set aside to drain on paper towels.
4. Drain the wok, wipe it clean and add the reserved oil. Gently stir-fry the Spice Paste over medium heat for 5 minutes until fragrant. Add the fried eggplants and basil, and season with sugar. Cook, stirring frequently, for 2 to 3 minutes, then serve.

SPECIAL NONYA FRIED RICE

This version of fried rice from a Nonya kitchen gets its distinctive flavour from the tiny dried salted fish used by Chinese cooks. Smaller than the usual Malay *ikan bilis*, they are sometimes called silverfish.

Serves 4
Preparation time: 15 mins
Cooking time: 10 mins

3 tablespoons oil
½ cup (80 g) very small dried silverfish or bits of salted fish
3 cloves garlic, minced
1 chicken breast (about 125 g/4 oz), diced
150 g (5 oz) medium fresh prawns, peeled and deveined
3 eggs, beaten
4 cups (800 g) cold cooked rice or leftover rice
1 tablespoon soy sauce
½ teaspoon salt
½ teaspoon pepper
¼ teaspoon sesame oil (optional)
1 handful (75 g) bean sprouts
2 spring onions, thinly sliced

1. Heat the oil in a wok and stir-fry the silverfish or salted fish until brown and crispy. Remove from the oil and set aside to drain.

2. In the same wok, gently stir-fry the garlic for a few seconds, then add the chicken and prawns, and stir-fry for 3 to 4 minutes. Increase the heat and add the eggs, stirring until the eggs are cooked.

3. Add the rice and stir-fry over high heat until the rice is heated through. Then add the rest of the ingredients and stir-fry for another minute. Add the crispy silverfish or salted fish and stir to mix well. Serve immediately.

> **NOTE:** Leftover rice kept overnight is preferred for any fried rice dish, as it is drier and firmer, and will result in a better textured fried rice dish.

BARBECUED CHICKEN WINGS

This is an easy dish to prepare that is a sure winner—roadside stalls all over Malaysia serve these wings at all hours, day and night.

Serves 4
Preparation time: 10 mins + 6 hours marination
Cooking time: 10 mins

1 kg (2 lbs) chicken wings
2 tablespoons oyster sauce
2 tablespoons honey
2 tablespoons rice wine or sherry
2 tablespoons soy sauce
1 tablespoon black soy sauce
1 teaspoon sesame oil
1 teaspoon freshly ground black pepper
¼ teaspoon salt (optional)

Mix all the ingredients and marinate the chicken wings for 6 hours or overnight. Cook over hot charcoal or in a preheated oven at 220°C (440°F) for 10 minutes until the chicken is cooked and golden brown.

NASI BOKHARI Spicy Rice with Chicken

Arab and Indian influences are evident in this richly flavoured rice, similar to a pilau or biryani. It is particularly popular in the northeastern states of Peninsular Malaysia.

Serves 4–6
Preparation time: 45 mins + marinate overnight
Cooking time: 1 hour

2 tablespoons tomato paste
½ cup (125 ml) evaporated milk or thick coconut milk
1 tablespoon lime juice
1 teaspoon salt
1 whole fresh chicken (about 1 kg/ 2 lbs), cut into serving pieces
3 tablespoons ghee or butter
2 cups (400 g) uncooked long-grain rice (preferably Basmati rice), rinsed and drained
2 cups (500 ml) water
Cucumber and Pineapple Achar (page 35), to serve

SPICE PASTE
½ cinnamon stick (2 cm/¾ in)
2 cloves
2 cardamom pods, husks discarded
2 star anise pods
3 tablespoons coriander seeds
2 tablespoons fennel seeds
1 tablespoon cumin seeds
1 teaspoon black peppercorns
1 teaspoon turmeric powder
1 teaspoon white poppy seeds (optional)
6 almonds, chopped
2 cm (¾ in) ginger, sliced
5 shallots, peeled and halved
2 cloves garlic, halved
½ cup (125 ml) water

RICE SPICE
2 shallots, peeled and halved
2 cloves garlic, peeled and halved
2½ cm (1 in) ginger, sliced
¼ cup (60 ml) water
1 tablespoon ghee or butter
½ cinnamon stick (2 cm/¾ in)
1 clove
1 star anise pod
1 cardamom pod
2 tablespoons evaporated milk or thick coconut milk
1 teaspoon salt

GARNISHES
½ cup (75 g) raisins
3 tablespoons Fried Shallots (page 33)
1 tablespoon roasted almond flakes

1. Prepare the Cucumber and Pineapple Achar by following the instructions on page 35.
2. Grind all the Spice Paste ingredients, then mix the Spice Paste with the tomato paste, milk, lime juice and salt. Coat the chicken pieces with this mixture and marinate overnight in the refrigerator for at least 3 hours.
3. Heat the ghee or butter in a pot and stir-fry the marinated chicken over low heat. Cook for 30 minutes until the meat is done, adding a little water if it threatens to burn. Remove the chicken from the pot and set aside on a platter. Reserve the gravy.
4. Prepare the Rice Spice by blending the shallots, garlic, ginger with water in a blender. Cook the purée in the ghee or butter for 5 minutes over medium heat in a small pot. Add the cinnamon, clove, star anise, cardamom, milk, salt and the reserved chicken gravy. Cook for another 3 minutes until fragrant.
5. Add the rice and stir to coat well with the spice gravy for 1 to 2 minutes, then add the water and stir again. Reduce the heat to low, cover and simmer for 20 minutes. Alternatively, cook the seasoned rice in a rice cooker.
6. Scoop the fluffy cooked rice onto a platter. Garnish with the raisins, Fried Shallots and roasted almond flakes, and serve with the spicy chicken and a bowl of Cucumber and Pineapple Achar on the side.

NOTE: Almonds are crunchy with a rich, delicate flavour. To prepare **roasted almond flakes**, purchase sliced raw almonds and roast them on a baking tray in a preheated over at 180°C (350°F) until golden, about 5 to 7 minutes. Almonds are sold shelled, unshelled, sliced, ground or chopped. Substitute pan-fried cashew nuts.

MALAYSIAN ROASTED CHICKEN RICE

Nasi Ayam

Chicken served with rice, chilli sauce and cucumber is one of the most popular coffee shop and hawker dishes in Malaysia. The Chinese version normally uses chicken simmered in stock, while this Malay recipe uses roast chicken.

Serves 4–6
Preparation time: 20 mins
Cooking time: 1 hour 10 mins

2 cups (400 g) uncooked rice, rinsed thoroughly and drained
2½ cm (1 in) ginger, peeled and bruised
3 cloves garlic, peeled and bruised
2 tablespoons butter
2 pandanus leaves, tied in a knot or ¼ teaspoon pandanus extract
Pinch of salt
4 cups (2 litres) water or chicken stock
3 tablespoons Fried Shallots (page 33)
1 cucumber, peeled and sliced, to serve
Chicken soup, to serve (optional)
Coriander leaves (cilantro), sliced, to garnish (optional)

Chilli Ginger Sauce (page 35), to serve
8 cloves garlic, ground to a paste, to serve (optional)
Black soy sauce, to serve (optional)

ROAST CHICKEN
1 whole fresh chicken (about 1 kg/ 2 lbs)
5 cm (2 in) ginger, sliced
4 shallots, peeled and halved
3 cloves garlic, peeled and halved
2 tablespoons oyster sauce
2 tablespoons soy sauce
1 tablespoon black soy sauce
1 tablespoon tomato ketchup
1 tablespoon Basic Chilli Sauce (page 35) or bottled chilli sauce
1 teaspoon chilli powder
1 teaspoon salt

1. Prepare the Chilli Ginger Sauce by following the instructions on page 35.
2. Prepare the Roast Chicken by first pricking the chicken all around with a fork to allow the seasonings to penetrate. Grind the ginger, shallots and garlic, and mix this together with the other ingredients. Rub this paste into the chicken skin and set aside to marinate for 4 hours or overnight in the refrigerator. Heat the oven to 220°C (425°F) and roast the chicken in the preheated oven for 30 to 40 minutes, then cut into serving pieces.
3. Cook the rice in a pot or rice cooker with the ginger, garlic, butter, pandanus leaves, salt and water. If using a pot, bring to a boil, reduce the heat and simmer, covered for 20 minutes until the rice is cooked.
4. Garnish the rice with Fried Shallots and serve with the chicken and cucumber. Also serve a small bowl of clear chicken soup garnished with coriander leaves, and small sauce bowls of the Chilli Ginger Sauce, garlic paste and black soy sauce on the side

YEN'S CRISPY BROWN NOODLES WITH GRAVY

This version of a Cantonese-style dish—deep-fried coils of crisp, light brown noodles bathed in a delicate and delicious sauce—is named after the chef who created it.

Serves 4
Preparation time: 30 mins
Cooking time: 10 mins

150 g (5 oz) dried wheat noodles
  (*yee mien*)
3 cups (300 g) mustard greens or
  spinach, washed
Oil for deep-frying
3 cloves garlic, minced
150 g (5 oz) medium fresh prawns,
  peeled and deveined
½ cup (150 g) chicken or pork, thinly
  sliced
2 cups (500 ml) water
1 tablespoon oyster sauce
1 tablespoon soy sauce
1 teaspoon black soy sauce
½ teaspoon sesame oil
½ teaspoon ground white pepper
1 tablespoon cornstarch mixed with
  3 tablespoons water
2 eggs, lightly beaten
Thinly sliced red chillies, to serve
Soy sauce, to serve

1. Place the dried noodles in a colander, sprinkle a few drops of cold water and set aside to soften for 10 minutes. Discard the hard ends of the mustard greens and cut the vegetable into 4-cm (1¾-in) lengths. If using spinach, rinse and cut into 4-cm (1¾-in) lengths.

2. Heat the oil in a wok over medium heat and deep-fry the noodles a handful at a time, turning them over until crispy and golden, about 1 minute. Drain the cooked noodles and set aside on a platter. Repeat with the remaining noodles.

3. Reserve 1 tablespoon of the oil in the wok and drain off the rest. Wipe the wok clean, return the reserved oil to the wok and stir-fry the garlic for a few seconds until golden brown. Add the prawns and chicken or pork and stir-fry until cooked, about 2 to 3 minutes. Add the water, oyster sauce, soy sauces and sesame oil. Season with the pepper and bring to a boil. Then add the mustard greens or spinach and simmer for a minute until the vegetable is wilted.

4. Add the cornstarch mixture and cook, stirring continuously, until the sauce thickens and clears, about 2 minutes. Then add the beaten eggs and cook until they set. Ladle into individual bowls and serve with the crunchy noodles. Alternatively, place the crunchy noodles in a bowl and ladle the cooked mixture over it. Serve hot, with a small bowl of sliced chilli and soy sauce on the side.

NOTE: Dried *yee mien* noodles are light beige in colour. They should have a firm and crunchy texture after cooking. The distinctive flavour of this noodle makes this simply named dish worth trying. Packets of dried *yee mien* noodles are available in Chinese provision shops.

INDIAN MEE GORENG Indian Fried Noodles

Although noodles were brought to Malaysia by the Chinese, all the other ethnic groups have enthusiastically adapted them to suit their tastes. This spicy dish—which you cannot find in India—is well-balanced by the sweetness of fresh tomatoes and tomato sauce.

Serves 6
Preparation time: 35 mins
Cooking time: 15 mins

4 tablespoons oil
1 cake firm or pressed tofu (250 g/
   8 oz total), drained and cubed
6–8 dried chillies, cut into lengths
   and soaked in warm water to
   soften, and ground to a paste
   or 3–5 tablespoons chilli powder
5 cloves garlic, minced
1 teaspoon *belachan* (dried prawn
   paste)
150 g (5 oz) boneless chicken, thinly
   sliced
150 g (5 oz) medium fresh prawns,
   peeled and deveined
400 g (12 oz) fresh yellow wheat
   noodles
2 cups (200 g) mustard greens
2 tablespoons soy sauce
3 tablespoons tomato sauce
½ teaspoon salt
½ cup (125 ml) chicken stock or
   ¼ teaspoon chicken stock
   granules mixed with ½ cup
   (125 ml) hot water
2 eggs, beaten
1 onion, diced
1 tomato, diced or 2 tablespoons
   tomato purée
1 red chilli, sliced
1 green chilli, sliced
2 cups (150 g) bean sprouts,
   tails discarded
½ teaspoon ground white pepper

GARNISHES
Coriander leaves (cilantro) or
   Chinese celery, coarsely chopped
Spring onions, sliced (optional)
Fried Shallots (page 33), (optional)
Small limes (*limau kasturi*), halved

1. Heat 2 tablespoons of the oil in a large wok and stir-fry the tofu cubes over medium heat until golden brown, about 7 minutes. Remove from the oil with a slotted spoon and set aside to drain on paper towels.
2. In the same wok, add the rest of the oil and stir-fry 3 to 5 tablespoons of the chilli paste or the chilli powder with the garlic and *belachan* for 3 minutes until fragrant. Add the chicken and stir-fry until it turns opaque, about 3 minutes. Then add the prawns and stir-fry until the prawns are cooked, another 2 minutes.
3. Add the noodles and mustard greens, mix well and cook for 1 minute. Then add the soy sauce, tomato sauce, salt and chicken stock, and cook for 3 minutes until the mixture is dry.
4. Push the noodles to one side of the wok with the spatula. Add the eggs and scramble. Then stir the noodles and the eggs together until the eggs are cooked. (Add a little more chicken stock for a moist Mee Goreng.)
5. Add the onion, tomato, fresh chillies and bean sprouts, and stir-fry for 3 minutes. Then add the fried tofu and mix well until heated through. Season with the ground pepper. Garnish with coriander leaves, spring onions, Fried Shallots and serve fresh limes on the side.

> **NOTE:** If preferred, substitute spinach or cabbage for the mustard greens.

FRIED KWAY TEOW Fried Rice Stick Noodles

A great food stall favourite using fresh rice flour noodles. The stall owner cooks one or two servings at a time in a large smoky wok and dishes it onto a serving plate just before serving. Always ensure that the shellfish is well cooked.

Serves 4
Preparation time: 30 mins
Cooking time: 10 mins

4 tablespoons oil
5 cloves garlic, minced
5–10 dried chillies, cut into lengths, soaked to soften, then ground to a paste
1 chicken breast (150 g/5 oz), thinly sliced
150 g (5 oz) medium fresh prawns, peeled and deveined
500 g (1 lb) fresh flat rice noodles (*kway teow*) or 250 g (8 oz) dried rice stick noodles
125 g (4 oz) *chye sim* (see note)
2 large eggs, beaten
2 tablespoons soy sauce
2 tablespoons black soy sauce
2 stalks garlic chives, minced
2 cups (150 g) bean sprouts, tails discarded
16–20 shelled fresh cockles, clams or mussels (about 60 g total) (optional)
¼ teaspoon salt

1. Heat the oil in a wok over high heat and stir-fry the garlic until golden brown, about 2 minutes. Add 1 to 2 tablespoons of the chilli paste and stir-fry for another minute. Add the chicken and prawns, and stir-fry for 3 minutes or until cooked.

2. Add the noodles, *chye sim* and eggs, and stir-fry over high heat for 2 minutes until the vegetable is wilted and the eggs are cooked. Add the soy sauces, chives, bean sprouts, cockles and season with the salt. Stir-fry until all the ingredients are thoroughly heated. Serve immediately.

> **NOTE:** Malaysian Chinese versions of this dish add pork, fried pork cracklings and sweet slices of *lap cheong* dried sausage. *Chye sim* is a leafy green vegetable with crunchy stems, which are similar in taste and texture to *bok choy*, which may be substituted. Mustard greens or sliced cabbage may also be used. Available in supermarkets in Asia, *chye sim* is now increasingly available in Western countries too.

LAKSA LEMAK Noodles in Spicy Coconut Gravy

This Nonya version of *laksa* from Malacca is a light and soupy, spicy noodle dish. It is infused with wild ginger buds to give a distinctly delicate fragrance. Although it takes some time to prepare, it is well worth the effort.

Serves 6
Preparation time: 1 hour
Cooking time: 30 mins

5 tablespoons oil
9 sprigs *laksa* leaves (*daun kesum*), sliced
3 wild ginger bud (*bunga kantan*), thinly sliced
5 cups (1¼ litres) water
1½ cups (375 ml) thick coconut milk or ¾ cup (185 ml) coconut cream mixed with ¾ cup (185 ml) water
1–2 teaspoons sugar
2 teaspoons salt
500 g (1 lb) fresh yellow wheat noodles (*mee*) or 250 g (8 oz) dried noodles, blanched and drained
1 whole chicken breast, poached in ½ cup (125 ml) water and thinly sliced
250 g (8 oz) medium fresh prawns, peeled and deveined and poached
1½ cups (75 g) bean sprouts, blanched

SPICE PASTE
5 candlenuts, roughly chopped
1 stalk lemongrass, thick bottom third only, outer layers removed, inner part sliced
2 cm (¾ in) galangal root, sliced
½ cm (¼ in) fresh turmeric root, sliced or ½ teaspoon turmeric powder
10 red chillies, deseeded and sliced
10 shallots, peeled and halved
3 cloves garlic, peeled and halved
1 teaspoon *belachan* (dried prawn paste)

GARNISHES
1 small cucumber, thinly sliced
3 eggs, beaten and fried into thin omelettes, then thinly sliced into shreds
2 red chillies, sliced
2 spring onions, thinly sliced
6 tablespoons Sambal Belachan (page 33), to serve
6 small limes (*limau kasturi*), halved, or lemon wedges, to serve

1. Prepare the Sambal Belachan by following the instructions on page 33.
2. Grind the Spice Paste ingredients in a mortar or blender, adding 1 tablespoon of the oil if necessary to keep the blades turning.
3. Heat the remaining oil in a saucepan over medium heat and gently stir-fry the Spice Paste for 5 to 7 minutes. Add 6 sprigs of the *laksa* leaves, 2 wild ginger buds and water, and bring to a boil. Then add the thick coconut milk and season with sugar and salt. Reduce the heat and simmer very gently, uncovered, for 10 to 15 minutes until the oil separates from the milk.
4. Blanch the fresh noodles in boiling water for a few seconds to heat through. If using dried noodles, boil them for about 7 minutes and drain or see packet instructions for preparation.
5. Divide the noodles, chicken, prawns and bean sprouts into 6 individual noodle bowls and top each bowl with the remaining *laksa* leaves and ginger bud slices. Pour the coconut gravy over the noodles and garnish with cucumber, eggs, chillies and spring onions. Serve with a small bowl of the Sambal Belachan and lime halves on the side.

NOTE: The coconut gravy can be prepared in advance and the garnish readied, although not sliced to ensure maximum fragrance and freshness. If fresh noodles are not available, use dried rice vermicelli (*beehoon*) or any dried Chinese wheat noodles.

PENANG LAKSA Penang-style Noodle Soup with Tamarind

There are two definite groups within Malaysia: those who prefer Laksa Lemak, a spicy noodle soup bathed in coconut milk gravy, and those who prefer the sour, fragrant Penang version which has a pronounced fishy flavour. Try both types of *laksa* and see which group you fall into. The Penang version is a bit like Thai Tom Yum Soup.

Serves 4–6
Preparation time: 1 hour
Cooking time: 35 mins

3 medium fresh mackerel or small tuna (about 600 g/1¼ lbs total), cleaned and left whole
8 cups (2 litres) water
4 tablespoons tamarind pulp, soaked in 1 cup (250 ml) water, mashed and then strained for juice
2 wild ginger buds (*bunga kantan*), sliced
3 sprigs *laksa* leaves (*daun kesum*), washed and sliced
2 tablespoons sugar
500 g (1 lb) fresh round rice noodles (*laksa* noodles) or 250 g (8 oz) dried rice noodles

SPICE PASTE
2 stalks lemongrass, thick bottom third only, outer layers removed, inner part sliced
2½ cm (1 in) fresh turmeric root, sliced, or 2 teaspoons turmeric powder
5 dried red chillies, soaked in warm water and cut into lengths
7 fresh red chillies, sliced
10 shallots, peeled and halved
1 teaspoon *belachan* (dried prawn paste)

GARNISHES
1 small cucumber, peeled, deseeded and thinly sliced
6 sprigs *laksa* leaves (*daun kesum*), sliced
Few sprigs mint, torn
1 large red onion, sliced
3 red chillies, sliced
½ fresh small pineapple, peeled and sliced into small pieces
4–6 hard-boiled quail eggs, halved or 3 hard-boiled chicken eggs, peeled and quartered (optional)
1 heaped teaspoon black prawn paste (*hay koh*), diluted in 2 tablespoons warm water

1. Simmer the cleaned fish in the water for 5 minutes until cooked. Remove the fish and set aside to cool. Strain the fish stock carefully and pour into a large pan with the tamarind juice, ginger buds, *laksa* leaves and sugar. When cool enough to handle, debone the fish and coarsely flake the flesh with a fork.
2. Grind the Spice Paste ingredients to a paste in a mortar or blender, adding a little oil if necessary to keep the blades turning. Add the Spice Paste to the pan with the fish stock. Add half of the flaked fish and simmer for 20 to 30 minutes.
3. Prepare the Garnishes.
4. Blanch the noodles in boiling water to heat through and drain. If using dried noodles, boil them for about 7 minutes and drain or see packet instructions for preparation. Divide the noodles into 6 serving bowls and ladle the fish stock to almost fill each bowl. Garnish each bowl with the rest of the flaked fish and a helping of the various Garnishes. Serve with a small bowl of the diluted black prawn paste (*hay koh*) on the side.

NOTE: If Chubb mackerel is not available, choose another dark, oily fish like tuna to ensure that the soup has its characteristic fishy taste. Use black prawn paste (*hay koh*) sparingly as it has strong fishy taste that takes a little getting used to. It is sold in packets or jars in supermarkets, sometimes under the Indonesian name *petis*.

FIERY CHICKEN CURRY DEVIL

This dish may be too spicy for some. The large amount of chillies makes the name "Devil's Curry" entirely appropriate for this Eurasian dish, which is based on the Indian Vindaloo Curry with its blending of spices and vinegar. A Malaysian touch is given with fresh lemongrass and galangal. To help reduce the heat, swirl a little plain yogurt into the curry or serve a small bowl of cold yogurt on the side.

Serves 6
Preparation time: 30 mins
Cooking time: 45 mins

4 tablespoons oil
5 cloves garlic, sliced
2 onions, quartered
5 cm (2 in) ginger, sliced into thin
    shreds
2 red chillies, halved lengthwise
1 chicken (about 1 kg/2 lbs), cut into
    serving pieces
500 g (1 lb) potatoes, peeled and
    halved
1½ teaspoons salt
1 teaspoon black soy sauce
2–4 tablespoons sugar
½ cup (125 ml) white vinegar
2–3 cups (500–750 ml) water

SPICE PASTE
1 teaspoon brown mustard seeds,
    soaked in water for 5 minutes
2 stalks lemongrass, thick bottom
    third only, outer layers removed,
    inner part sliced
2½ cm (1 in) galangal root, sliced
3 cm (1¼ in) fresh turmeric root,
    sliced or 2½ teaspoons turmeric
    powder
15 dried chillies, cut into lengths,
    soaked to soften and deseeded
30 shallots, peeled and halved

1. Grind the Spice Paste ingredients, adding a little oil if necessary to keep the blades turning.
2. Heat 2 tablespoons of the oil in a wok and stir-fry the garlic, onions, ginger and chillies for 2 minutes. Drain the fried mixture and set aside.
3. Stir-fry the ground Spice Paste with the remaining 2 tablespoons oil in the wok over medium to high heat for 5 to 7 minutes. Add the chicken, potatoes, salt and soy sauce, and cook for 10 minutes. Then add the sugar, vinegar and water. Add a little more vinegar for a more sour curry if preferred. Reduce the heat and simmer, uncovered, for 20 minutes until the chicken is cooked.
4. Add the reserved fried mixture (from step 2) and stir to mix well. Transfer the curry to a platter and serve hot with freshly cooked rice or Roti Canai (page 41).

NOTE: To reduce the spiciness of the dish, reduce the dried chillies, cut them into lengths before soaking, and discard the seeds which fall to the bottom of the bowl. If the dish is too hot, increase the amount of sugar called for in the recipe to reduce the heat.

SPICY KELANTANESE BARBECUED CHICKEN

Ayam Percik

It's not surprising that this beautifully seasoned chicken, barbecued over a charcoal fire, is so popular and is sold at roadside food stalls and markets all over the northeastern state of Kelantan.

Serves 4
Preparation time: 20 mins + 1 hour marination
Cooking time: 15 mins (for sambal) + 5–10 mins grilling

1 chicken (about 1 kg/2 lbs), quartered or 5 whole chicken legs
4 tablespoons oil
1 slice *asam gelugur* or 2 teaspoons tamarind pulp
4 stalks lemongrass, thick bottom third only, outer layers removed, inner part bruised

1 cup (250 ml) water
1 cup (250 ml) thick coconut milk or ½ cup (125 ml) coconut cream mixed with ½ cup (125 ml) water
½ tablespoon sugar
1 teaspoon salt

MARINADE
1 teaspoon turmeric powder
1 teaspoon chilli powder
1 tablespoon sugar
½ teaspoon salt

SPICE PASTE
4 candlenuts, roughly chopped
2 cm (¾ in) ginger, sliced
9 dried chillies, cut into lengths and soaked in warm water
3 red chillies, sliced
6 cloves garlic, peeled and halved
5 shallots, peeled and halved

NOTE: The chicken can be prepared in advance and kept in the refrigerator for up to 24 hours before barbecuing.

1. Mix the Marinade ingredients together and rub into the chicken. Then set the chicken aside to marinate for 1 hour.
2. Grind the Spice Paste ingredients to a paste in a mortar or blender, adding a little oil if necessary to keep the blades turning.
3. Heat the oil in a wok and stir-fry the Spice Paste over medium heat for 5 minutes until fragrant. Add the *asam gelugur* or tamarind pulp and lemongrass, and stir-fry for another 3 minutes. Add the water, stir and cook for 3 minutes.

4. Add the chicken, coconut milk, sugar and salt. Reduce the heat and simmer over low heat for 20 to 30 minutes. Remove from the heat and transfer the chicken to a plate. Reserve the gravy.
5. Barbecue the chicken over a low charcoal fire or under a grill, basting frequently with the gravy until the chicken is cooked, about 5 to 10 minutes on each side. Serve hot, topped with the remaining gravy as part of a rice-based meal.

LONTONG Compressed Rice Cakes

Lontong makes a great substitute for rice. You can also buy prepared cylinders of Lontong wrapped in banana leaves from Malay shops. Simply slice and serve.

Serves 4
Preparation time: 5 mins
Cooking time: 2 hours 30 mins

½ cup (100 g) uncooked long-grain rice, washed
2 pieces banana leaf about 35 x 30 cm (14 x 12 in) or 1 cheesecloth about 60 cm x 60 cm (24 in x 24 in)
Kitchen string

1. Place a banana leaf over the other and roll into a cylinder about 6 cm (2½ in) in diameter. Seal the lower end with a toothpick and add the rice into the roll. Fold the leaf over and secure the top end of the roll, leaving two-thirds of the roll empty for the rice to expand during cooking. Place the roll in a pot of boiling water, cover and simmer very gently for 2 to 2½ hours. Then remove from the pot and cool to room temperature before serving.
2. If using cheesecloth, fold the cloth in half, place the rice on the cloth and roll it up. Seal one end with a kitchen string. Then seal the other end of the cloth with another piece of kitchen string, leaving enough room in the cloth to hold 2 times the amount of uncooked rice. Then proceed to cook as described above.

MALAYSIAN CHICKEN SATAY Sate Ayam

The tantalising aroma of seasoned mutton, beef or chicken cooking over a charcoal fire, anointed from time to time with oil spread with a "brush" of fragrant lemongrass, is irresistible. It's no wonder this Malay dish is an all-time favourite.

Makes 12 sticks
Preparation time: 30 mins +
    12 hours marination
Cooking time: 10 mins

½ teaspoon chilli powder
2 tablespoons sugar
½ teaspoon salt
1 teaspoon turmeric powder
4 chicken legs and thighs, deboned and cut into 2-cm (¾-in) cubes

NOTE: *Ketupat* are compressed rice cakes similar to Lontong, (page 81). They are packed in beautifully woven cases of coconut leaves or *daun palas* (see photo) and boiled in water. The rice takes the shape of the case and is usually served quartered. These traditional festive cakes dress every table during many celebrations in Malaysia. Ketupat are sold in many Malay food stores.

12 skewers soaked in water for 1 hour
1 stalk lemongrass, thick end lightly bruised, for brushing
Oil for brushing
Satay Sauce (see recipe below), for dipping
Cucumber, sliced, to serve
Onion, sliced, to serve
Ketupat, quartered, to serve (optional, see note)

SPICE PASTE
1 tablespoon coriander seeds
2 stalks lemongrass, thick bottom third only, outer layers removed, inner part sliced
5 shallots, peeled and halved
2 cloves garlic, peeled and halved
2 tablespoons oil

1. Grind the Spice Paste ingredients in a mortar or blender, adding the oil to keep the blades turning. Mix the paste with the chilli powder, sugar, salt and turmeric powder, and marinate the chicken cubes for at least 12 hours.

2. Thread 4 to 5 pieces of the marinated chicken onto each skewer until all the chicken pieces are used up. Grill the chicken over a hot charcoal fire, constantly brushing with a stalk of lemongrass dipped in the oil. Turn the skewers frequently to prevent the meat from burning. The chicken should be slightly charred on the outside and just cooked on the inside. Alternatively, grill the chicken under an oven broiler for 10 minutes on each side.

3. Serve with a bowl of Satay Sauce and sliced cucumber, raw onion and Ketupat or boiled rice on the side.

SATAY SAUCE

Makes 1 cup
Preparation time: 25 mins
Cooking time: 10 mins

4 tablespoons oil
½ cup (75 g) roasted peanuts, skins discarded and coarsely ground
½ tablespoon tamarind pulp, soaked in 2 tablespoons water, mashed and then strained to obtain juice
½ cup (125 ml) water
¼ teaspoon salt
1 tablespoon sugar

SPICE PASTE
1 tablespoon coriander seeds
½ teaspoon cumin seeds

2 stalks lemongrass, thick bottom third only, outer layers removed, inner part sliced
1½ cm (¾ in) galangal root, sliced
4 dried chillies, cut into lengths and soaked in warm water
3 cloves garlic, peeled and halved
2 shallots, peeled and halved

1. Grind the Spice Paste ingredients in a mortar or blender, adding a little oil if necessary to keep the blades turning.

2. Heat the oil in a saucepan over medium to high heat and stir-fry the Spice Paste for 3 to 5 minutes until fragrant. Add the peanuts, tamarind juice and water, and season with salt and sugar. Reduce the heat to low and cook for another 3 minutes, stirring constantly, then remove from the heat. Transfer the sauce to a bowl and serve warm or at room temperature.

NOTE: You may substitute ½ cup (6 tablespoons) crunchy peanut butter for the crushed peanuts. Add the peanut butter to the sauce and mix thoroughly, then remove from the heat. Satay Sauce can be made in large quantities and kept in the the refrigerator for 2–3 weeks or frozen for 3 months.

NONYA CHICKEN CURRY WITH FRAGRANT LIME LEAVES

Ayam Limau Purut

The charm of this Nonya curry comes from its aromatic fresh herbs and seasonings.

Serves 4–6
Preparation time: 30 mins
Cooking time: 30 mins

4 tablespoons oil
1 chicken (about 1 kg/2 lbs), cut into
   serving pieces
1 slice *asam gelugur* (optional)
½ cup (125 ml) water
1 cup (250 ml) thick coconut milk
   or ½ cup (125 ml) coconut cream
   mixed with ½ cup (125 ml) water
4 kaffir lime leaves
1½ teaspoons salt
1–2 tablespoons fresh lime juice

SPICE PASTE
3 cm (1¼ in) galangal root, sliced
1 stalk lemongrass, thick bottom
   third only, outer layers removed,
   inner part sliced
8–10 red chillies, sliced
2 medium onions, quartered
3 cloves garlic, peeled and halved
1 teaspoon turmeric powder

1. Grind the Spice Paste ingredients in a mortar or blender, adding a little oil if necessary to keep the blades turning.
2. Heat the oil in a wok and stir-fry the Spice Paste over medium heat for 7 minutes, until fragrant. Add the chicken, *asam gelugur* and water, and simmer for 10 minutes until the chicken is half cooked.
3. Add the coconut milk and lime leaves, and simmer, uncovered, for a further 10 minutes until the chicken is tender. Season with salt and fresh lime juice.

NONYA SAYUR LEMAK Vegetables in Coconut Milk

A Nonya adaptation of the popular Malay-style vegetable dish simmered in a lightly spiced coconut milk.

Serves 4–6
Preparation time: 40 mins
Cooking time: 30 mins

1 carrot
1 slender Asian eggplant
¼ small *bangkuang* (jicama), peeled
3 long beans or 12 green beans
¼ small cabbage
1 cake firm tofu (250 g/8 oz), drained
Oil for shallow-frying (about 3 tablespoons)
1½ (375 ml) cups water
1½ cups (375 ml) thick coconut milk
   or ¾ cup (185 ml) coconut cream
   mixed with ¾ cup (185 ml) water
1 teaspoon salt

SPICE PASTE
3 candlenuts, roughly chopped
1 teaspoon dried prawns, soaked
   for 5 minutes in warm water and
   drained
2 red chillies, sliced
5 shallots, peeled and halved
½ teaspoon turmeric powder
½ teaspoon *belachan* (dried prawn
   paste)

> **NOTE:** Use a variety of veg-
> etables but not green leafy veg-
> etables as they will wilt and turn
> yellow. Serve this dish hot with
> Lontong (page 81) and garnish
> with Coconut Serunding (page
> 57) to make **Sayur Lontong**, a
> popular Malaysian breakfast.

1. Grind the Spice Paste ingredients in a mortar or blender, adding a little oil if necessary to keep the blades turning, and set aside.
2. Quarter the carrot and eggplant lengthwise, and cut into 4-cm (1½-in) long strips. Slice the *bangkuang*, long beans or green beans into strips of the same length. Then slice the cabbage into bite sized chunks.
3. Pan-fry the tofu in the oil in a large wok over medium heat until golden brown, about 3 minutes on each side. Remove from the oil and set aside to drain on paper towels. Let it cool, then cut the tofu into 8 pieces.
4. In the same wok, stir-fry the Spice Paste over medium heat for 7 minutes until fragrant. Add the water and coconut milk, and slowly bring to a boil. Add the prepared vegetables and season with the salt. Stir gently and bring to a boil. Reduce the heat, add the tofu and simmer, uncovered, for 5 minutes until the vegetables are just cooked. Serve hot.

FRAGRANT BEEF RENDANG Beef Stewed in Coconut and Spices

No festive occasion is complete without this rich Sumatran dish where beef is cooked to melt-in-the-mouth tenderness in a fragrant coconut gravy. This *rendang* actually tastes better the next day!

Serves 4–6
Preparation time: 30 mins
Cooking time: 2 hours 10 mins

1 cup (100 g) grated fresh coconut
4 tablespoons oil
1 stalk lemongrass, thick bottom
   third only, outer layers removed,
   inner part bruised
½ cinnamon stick (3 cm/1¼ in)
2 cloves
4 star anise pods
2 cardamom pods
500 g (1 lb) topside or stewing beef,
   cubed
1 cup (250 ml) thick coconut milk
   or ½ cup (125 ml) coconut cream
   mixed with ½ cup (125 ml) water
1 slice *asam gelugur* or 2 teaspoons
   dried tamarind pulp soaked in
   ½ cup (125 ml) water, mashed and
   strained for juice
2 kaffir lime leaves, very thinly sliced
1 turmeric leaf, very thinly sliced
   (optional)
1½ teaspoons sugar
1 tablespoon soy sauce

SPICE PASTE
2 stalks lemongrass, thick bottom
   third only, outer layers removed,
   inner part sliced
2 cm (¾ in) galangal root, sliced
2 cm (¾ in) ginger, sliced
10 dried chillies, cut into lengths and
   soaked in warm water
2 shallots, peeled and halved
2 cloves garlic, peeled and halved

1. Dry-fry the grated coconut in a wok or skillet, stirring constantly over low heat for 10 minutes until brown. Grind the coconut in a mortar while it is still hot and crispy. If a little oil oozes out, mix it into the coconut. Set aside.
2. Grind the Spice Paste ingredients in a mortar or blender, adding a little oil if necessary to keep the blades turning.
3. Heat the oil over medium heat in a saucepan, add the Spice Paste, lemongrass, cinnamon, cloves, star anise and cardamom pods, and stir-fry for 5 to 7 minutes until fragrant.
4. Add the beef, coconut milk and *asam gelugur* or tamarind juice and stir. Reduce the heat and simmer, uncovered, stirring frequently until the meat is almost cooked, about 45 minutes.
5. Add the lime and turmeric leaves, and the ground coconut, and season with the sugar and soy sauce. Simmer until the meat is very tender and the gravy has dried up, about 1 to 1½ hours. Serve with rice.

SOUTHERN INDIAN MUTTON CURRY

Mutton is a popular meat with both Indians and Malays, who often use goat or lamb instead. This is a typical spicy southern Indian curry with hearty potatoes adding a pleasant wholesome flavour. It is usually enjoyed with crusty french bread.

Serves 6
Preparation time: 15 mins
Cooking time: 1 hour 20 mins

500 g (1 lb) boneless lamb or
    mutton, cubed
4 cups (1 litre) water
4 tomatoes, cut into wedges
2–4 tablespoons chilli powder
1 teaspoon turmeric powder
¼ cup (60 ml) oil
1½ cups (250 g) shallots, sliced
1 cm (½ in) ginger, sliced
7 cloves garlic, sliced
4 potatoes (about 500 g/1 lb),
    peeled and cubed
2 sprigs curry leaves
1 teaspoon salt
1 teaspoon sugar

1. Bring the meat, water, tomatoes, chilli and turmeric powders to a boil in a pot. Reduce the heat and simmer, partially covered, for 45 minutes or until the meat is tender.
2. Heat the oil in a skillet and stir-fry the shallots, ginger and garlic over medium heat for about 7 minutes. Add this mixture to the pot with the meat.
3. Then add the potatoes and cook until they are tender and the liquid has reduced by half, about 20 minutes.
4. Add the curry leaves and cook until the sauce thickens, about 10 minutes. Then season with the salt and sugar. Serve immediately with slices of bread or rice.

> NOTE: This is a very spicy curry, so adjust the amount of chilli powder called for in the recipe to suit your tolerance.

CHICKEN CURRY WITH COCONUT

The use of cinnamon and star anise gives a robust flavour to this Indian chicken curry.

Serves 4–6
Preparation time: 25 mins
Cooking time: 30 mins

10–15 dried chillies, cut into lengths,
    soaked to soften, then ground to a
    paste in a mortar or blender
7 tablespoons chicken curry powder
3 tablespoons ghee or oil
2 cinnamon sticks (each 5 cm/2 in)
3 star anise pods
Handful of curry leaves
5 small potatoes (500 g/1 lb total),
    peeled and halved
1 chicken (about 1 kg/2 lbs), cut into
    serving pieces
2½ cups (625 ml) thin coconut milk
    or ¾ cup (175 ml) coconut cream
    mixed with 1½ cups (375 ml)
    water
1½ teaspoons salt
2 teaspoons sugar

SPICE PASTE
2½ cm (1 in) ginger, sliced
15 shallots, peeled and halved
4 cloves garlic, peeled and halved

1. Grind the Spice Paste ingredients in a mortar or blender, adding a little oil if necessary to keep the blades turning, and set aside. Mix the ground chillies and curry powder together with ½ cup (125 ml) water to form a paste.
2. Melt the ghee in a large pot and stir-fry the ground Spice Paste over medium heat for 3 to 5 minutes. Add the chilli-curry powder paste and continue to stir-fry until fragrant, about 3 minutes.
3. Add the cinnamon sticks, star anise, curry leaves, potatoes and chicken, and cook until the chicken is half done, about 15 minutes. Add the coconut milk and season with the salt and sugar. Reduce the heat and simmer for 20 minutes until the meat is cooked and the oil separates from the milk. Serve hot with freshly cooked white rice.

ROTI JALA Lacy Indian Pancakes

These lovely lacy pancakes are an ideal accompaniment to dishes with lots of rich gravy. They are particularly popular during the Muslim fasting month and special occasions.

Serves 4
Preparation time: 10 mins
Cooking time: 25 mins

2 cups (300 g) flour
2 cups (500 ml) fresh milk
1 egg
1/2 teaspoon salt
1/4 teaspoon turmeric powder
1 tablespoon oil
2 tablespoons ghee or butter

1. Sift the flour into a large bowl. Beat the milk and egg together, and mix with the flour, salt and turmeric powder to form a smooth batter. Strain the batter to remove any lumps. Then add the oil, stir and set aside.

2. Heat a non-stick skillet and brush the surface with the ghee or butter. Pour a ladleful of the batter into a special Roti Jala funnel (see note) and make quick circular movements over the skillet to form a lacy pattern.
3. Cook the pancake until it sets, about 1 to 2 minutes, and set aside. Repeat until all the batter is used up.

NOTE: A Roti Jala funnel (see photo) is a cup with four spouts. An alternative is a plastic sauce dispenser with a reasonably wide hole.

PRAWN SAMBAL Sambal Udang

Serves 4–6
Preparation time: 25 mins
Cooking time: 10 mins

1/4 cup (60 ml) oil
2 tablespoons shaved palm sugar or brown sugar
1 1/2 teaspoons salt
3 tablespoons thick coconut milk
4 tablespoons lime juice
500 g (1 lb) medium fresh prawns, peeled and deveined

SPICE PASTE
1 candlenut, roughly chopped
5 dried chillies, cut into lengths and soaked in warm water, then drained
2–5 red chillies, sliced and deseeded
1 cm (1/2 in) ginger, sliced
1 red onion, sliced
5 cloves garlic, peeled and halved
2 tablespoons water

1. Grind the Spice Paste ingredients to a paste in a mortar or blender, adding a little oil if necessary to keep the blades turning.
2. Heat the oil in a wok and stir-fry the Spice Paste over medium to high heat for 5 to 7 minutes until fragrant. Add the palm sugar, salt and coconut milk, and bring to a boil. Add the lime juice and prawns, and cook over high heat for 3 minutes until the prawns are cooked. Serve with rice or Roti Jala.

SPICY PRAWNS

A "sarong" of fragrant pandanus or banana leaf is optional but adds a decorative touch and a subtle fragrance to the prawns.

Serves 4
Preparation time: 20 mins
Cooking time: 5 mins

500 g (1 lb) large fresh prawns, sliced lengthwise and gently deveined
$\frac{1}{2}$ teaspoon salt
$\frac{1}{2}$ teaspoon pepper
1 tablespoon lime juice
$\frac{1}{2}$ cup (125 ml) thick coconut milk or $\frac{1}{4}$ cup (60 ml) coconut cream
    mixed with $\frac{1}{4}$ cup (60 ml) water
$\frac{1}{2}$ tablespoon shaved palm sugar of brown sugar
Pandanus leaves or banana leaf torn into 4-cm (1$\frac{1}{2}$-in) wide strips, for
    wrapping the prawns
Basic Chilli Sauce (page 35) or Chilli Ginger Sauce (page 35)

SPICE PASTE
2 candlenuts, roughly chopped
2 cm ($\frac{3}{4}$ in) galangal root, sliced
6 red chillies, sliced
8 shallots, peeled and halved
5 cloves garlic, peeled and halved
1 teaspoon turmeric powder
1 teaspoon *belachan* (dried prawn paste)

1. Prepare the Basic Chilli Sauce or Chilli Ginger Sauce by following the instructions on page 35.
2. Season the prawns with the salt, pepper and lime juice.
3. Grind the Spice Paste ingredients in a mortar or blender, adding a little oil if necessary to keep the blades turning. Mix the Spice Paste with the coconut milk and palm sugar. Add this mixture to the seasoned prawns, mix well and set aside to marinate for 4 to 6 hours.
4. Wrap the middle segment of each prawn with a pandanus leaf or a strip of banana leaf and secure with a toothpick (see photo). Barbecue the prawns over very hot charcoal or cook under a grill for 2 to 3 minutes on each side, taking care not to overcook the prawns. Serve immediately with a small bowl of the Basic Chilli Sauce or Chilli Ginger Sauce on the side.

BUTTER PRAWNS

A relatively recent Malaysian creation, this dish combines traditional Malay, Chinese, Indian and Western ingredients, highlighting the fresh seafood available all year from the waters surrounding Malaysia.

Serves 4–6
Preparation time: 20 mins
Cooking time: 7 mins

600 g (1¼ lbs) large fresh prawns
Oil for deep-frying
2–3 tablespoons butter
15 *chili padi* (bird's-eye chillies),
    bruised or left whole
10–15 curry leaves
3 cloves garlic, minced
½ teaspoon salt
1 cup (100 g) fresh grated coconut,
    dry-fried until golden brown
1 teaspoon rice wine
1 tablespoon sugar
½ teaspoon soy sauce

1. Slice the prawns lengthwise, through the shells, and gently devein them. Then trim the feelers and the legs. Then pat the prawns dry with paper towels and deep-fry them in hot oil until golden brown, about 3 minutes. Remove from the oil and set aside to drain.
2. Melt the butter in a saucepan and sauté the chillies, curry leaves, garlic with the salt for 2 minutes. Add the prawns, grated coconut, wine, sugar and soy sauce, and stir-fry briskly over high heat for 1 to 2 minutes. Serve immediately.

BLACK PEPPER CRAB

This is a truly original Malaysian dish—begin with fresh crabs and seasonings, spice it up with black pepper and curry leaves, enrich with butter and finally, toss in some chili padi for a knock–out result.

Serves 4–6
Preparation time: 30 mins
Cooking time: 25 mins

2 tablespoons dried prawns
1½–2 kg (3–4 lbs) fresh crabs
¼ cup (60 ml) oil
2 tablespoons butter
2 shallots, minced
7 cloves garlic, minced
1 tablespoon fermented soybean
    paste (*tau cheo*), mashed
3½ tablespoons black peppercorns,
    cracked or coarsely ground
½ cup (20 g) curry leaves
10 red or green *chili padi* (bird's-eye
    chillies), whole
3 tablespoons sugar
2 tablespoons black soy sauce
1 tablespoon oyster sauce
¼ cup (60 ml) water

1. Rinse and drain the dried prawns. Then dry roast them in a skillet for 2 to 3 minutes. Allow to cool, then grind coarsely in a mortar or blender.
2. To prepare the crabs, lift the triangular-shaped "apron" on the underside of the crab. Insert your thumb between the body and topshell at the rear of the crab and pull the topshell off. Discard the grey gills on either side of the body and any spongy grey matter. Clean the crab thoroughly, then rinse and drain. Quarter the crabs and crack the claws so the spices can penetrate.
3. Heat the oil in a wok and stir-fry the crabs over high heat for 5 minutes. Cover the wok and let the crabs cook for another 5 minutes. Remove from the heat and set the crabs aside on a rack to allow the oil to drain.
4. In the same wok, melt the butter in the remaining oil over medium heat. Stir-fry the shallots, garlic, fermented soybean paste, dried prawns, black peppercorns, curry leaves and chillies until fragrant, about 3 to 5 minutes. Add the crabs and the remaining ingredients. Cook for 5 to 10 minutes until the crabs are pink and cooked through.

PORTUGUESE BAKED FISH

This fish creation is from Malacca's Portuguese Settlement, many of whose ancestors hailed from Goa in India or Galle in southern Sri Lanka. It blends Malay spices and herbs with Chinese soy sauce for a unique taste.

Serves 4
Preparation time: 25 mins
Cooking time: 10 mins

5 tablespoons oil
2 teaspoons chilli powder
5 kaffir lime leaves, very thinly sliced
1 teaspoon sesame oil
½ teaspoon soy sauce
½ teaspoon salt
¼ teaspoon sugar
1 whole seabass or grouper (about
    750 g/1½ lbs) or 6 white fish fillets
Banana leaf, for wrapping
Aluminium foil, for wrapping

SPICE PASTE
5 candlenuts, roughly chopped
1 cm (½ in) galangal root, sliced
2 stalks lemongrass, thick bottom
    third only, outer layers removed,
    inner part sliced
6 red chillies, sliced
3 onions, quartered
1 scant teaspoon *belachan* (dried
    prawn paste)
½–¾ cup (125–175 ml) water

1. Grind the Spice Paste ingredients to a paste in a mortar or blender, adding a little oil if necessary to keep the blades turning. Heat the oil in a skillet over medium heat and stir-fry the Spice Paste with the chilli powder and lime leaves for 5 to 7 minutes until fragrant. Add the sesame oil, soy sauce, salt and sugar, and mix well. Remove from the heat and set aside to cool.

2. If using a whole fish, remove the scales, gills and clean the fish. Use a sharp knife to fillet the fish, starting from the tail to the head. Then gently flatten the fish with your hand and slice the flesh away from the backbone.

3. Preheat the oven to 200°C (400°F). Rub the cooled cooked spices over the fish, pushing it well into the slits to allow the spices to penetrate. If using fish fillets, coat generously on both sides with the spices.

4. Cut a large piece of banana leaf and brush with a little oil. Place the spice-covered fish on the banana leaf and fold it into a package. Wrap the banana leaf package again in foil and seal the ends. If using fillets, wrap each fillet individually. Bake in a preheated oven for 20 minutes, or barbecue or grill for 10 minutes on each side until cooked. Serve the fish immediately, straight from the fire to the table.

NOTE: The Spice Paste can be prepared several hours in advance and rubbed into the fish just before cooking.

INDIAN FISH CURRY

Many Indian fish curries include eggplants and okra, vegetables which seem to have a particular affinity with Indian spices and fish.

Serves 6–8
Preparation time: 40 mins
Cooking time: 35 mins

6 fish fillets (750 g/1½ lbs total), rubbed with ½ teaspoon salt and 2 teaspoons turmeric powder
2 slender Asian eggplants, halved lengthwise, cut into 3 pieces and patted dry
Oil for deep-frying

5 tablespoons oil
1 teaspoon brown mustard seeds
1 teaspoon fenugreek seeds
1 cinnamon stick
5 cardamom pods, bruised
7 dried chillies, left whole
9 shallots, sliced
4 large onions, sliced
8 cloves garlic, sliced
2½ cm (1 in) ginger, sliced
7 tablespoons fish curry powder

1 tablespoon chilli powder
1½ teaspoons turmeric powder
3 heaped tablespoons tamarind pulp mashed in 1 cup (250 ml) water, squeezed and strained for juice
5 cups (1¼ litres) water
7 okras, stalks and tips discarded
1 large tomato, cut into wedges
2 sprigs curry leaves
1 tablespoon sugar
1 tablespoon salt

1. Deep-fry the fish fillets in hot oil in a wok until golden brown, about 3 minutes. Remove from the heat and set aside to drain. Repeat with the eggplants.
2. Heat 5 tablespoons of oil in a pot over medium heat and add the mustard seeds. When the seeds pop, add the fenugreek, cinnamon and cardamom, and gently stir-fry for 2 minutes. Then add the dried chillies, shallots, onions, garlic and ginger, and stir-fry for 5 minutes until fragrant. Add the curry, chilli and turmeric powders, and stir-fry for another 3 minutes.
3. Add the tamarind juice and water, and bring to a boil. Add the eggplants, okras, tomato and curry leaves, reduce the heat and simmer for 10 minutes. Add the fish and season with the sugar and salt. Simmer for another 5 minutes until the fish is cooked. Remove from the heat and serve immediately.

NOTE: The curry sauce, eggplants and fish can be cooked in advance and kept separately. Just before serving, simmer the curry sauce with the eggplants and vegetables, and cook for 10 minutes. Then add the fish and heat through.

BUTTER RICE

Serves 6–8
Preparation time: 15 mins
Cooking time: 30 mins

2 tablespoons ghee or butter
½ teaspoon mustard seeds
1 cinnamon stick
3 cardamom pods, bruised
2 cloves
5 shallots, sliced
2 green chillies, deseeded and sliced
2 cups (400 g) uncooked long-grain rice (Basmati rice preferred), washed and drained
3 cups (750 ml) water
1 teaspoon salt

GARNISHES
1 tablespoon ghee or butter
10 raisins
10 cashew nuts
4 shallots, peeled and sliced

1. Heat the ghee or butter in a pot over medium heat and cook the mustard seeds until they pop. Add the cinnamon, cardamom and cloves, and stir-fry for 1 minute. Add the shallots and chillies, and cook for another 3 minutes.
2. Add the rice and stir to coat with the spices for 1 to 2 minutes, then add the water and salt, and stir again. Reduce the heat to low, cover and simmer for 15 to 20 minutes until the rice is cooked. Alternatively, cook the seasoned rice in a rice cooker.
3. To prepare the Garnishes, heat the ghee in a skillet over medium heat and stir-fry the raisins until they plump up, about 1 minute. Remove from the oil and set aside. Then repeat with the cashew nuts. Stir-fry the shallots for 3 minutes and set aside.
4. Sprinkle the Garnishes on the rice and serve hot.

EURASIAN SALTED FISH AND PINEAPPLE CURRY

Salted fish is popular in Malaysia, and not just when fresh fish are unavailable, like during the monsoon storms but anytime at all. This Eurasian curry uses good quality dried fish cut into bite-sized chunks.

Serves 4
Preparation time: 20 mins
Cooking time: 20 mins

1 small just-ripe pineapple (about 500 g/1 lb)
3 tablespoons oil
125 g (4 oz) salted fish, soaked for ½ hour in warm water, drained, cut into bite-sized chunks and patted dry
½ cup (125 ml) water
½ cup (125 ml) thick coconut milk or ¼ cup (60 ml) coconut cream mixed with ¼ cup (60 ml) water
¼ teaspoon salt

SPICE PASTE
2 stalks lemongrass, thick bottom third only, outer layers removed, inner part sliced
2½ cm (1 in) galangal root, sliced
2½ cm (1 in) fresh turmeric root, sliced
3 red chillies, sliced
6 shallots, peeled and halved
½ teaspoon *belachan* (dried prawn paste)

1. Peel the pineapple and discard the eyes. Quarter the pineapple, remove the fibrous core and rinse. Slice the flesh into long thick strips, then into small triangular pieces. Blend half the pineapple flesh with ¼ cup (60 ml) water to a pulp and set aside.
2. Grind all the Spice Paste ingredients in a mortar or blender, adding a little oil if necessary to keep the blades turning.
3. Heat the oil in a wok over medium heat and fry the salted fish until light golden brown, about 5 minutes. Remove the fish from the wok and set aside. Add the Spice Paste to the same wok and stir-fry gently over medium heat for 5 minutes until fragrant. Return the fish to the wok, add the pineapple pieces and stir to coat them with the paste. Then add the reserved pineapple pulp, the rest of the water and the coconut milk. Reduce the heat and simmer gently for about 10 to 15 minutes until the pineapple is tender and the oil separates from the milk. Season with the salt.
4. Remove from the heat and transfer the curry to a serving bowl. Serve with freshly cooked white rice.

> **NOTE:** Blending half the pineapple into a pulp imparts a lovely sweet flavour to the curry gravy. If salted fish is unavailable, substitute 500 g (1 lb) fresh prawns, shelled and deveined.

PINEAPPLE AND PRAWN CURRY WITH COCONUT

Nenas Lemak

Pineapple perfectly complements the prawns and spices as shown in this piquant curry.

Serves 4–6
Preparation time: 25 mins
Cooking time: 20 mins

½ small just-ripe pineapple (about 250 g/8 oz)
2 cups (250 ml) water
4 tablespoons oil
200 g (7 oz) medium fresh prawns, peeled and deveined
1½ cups (375 ml) thick coconut milk or ¾ cup (175 ml) coconut cream mix with ¾ cup (175 ml) water
¾ teaspoon salt

SPICE PASTE
½ teaspoon turmeric powder
2 stalks lemongrass, thick bottom third only, outer layers removed, inner part sliced
6 red chillies, sliced

8 shallots, peeled and halved
2 cloves garlic, peeled and halved
½ teaspoon *belachan* (dried prawn paste)

1. Peel the pineapple and discard the eyes. Quarter the pineapple, remove the fibrous core and rinse in water. Slice the flesh into long thick strips, then cut into small triangular pieces.
2. Grind the Spice Paste ingredients in a blender with ¼–½ cup (60–125 ml) water to keep the blades turning. Heat the oil in a saucepan over medium heat and stir-fry the Spice Paste for 5 minutes until fragrant. Add the pineapple and stir-fry for another 5 minutes, then add the rest of the water and cook for another 10 minutes until the pineapple is soft.
3. Add the prawns, coconut milk and season with the salt. Reduce the heat and simmer, uncovered, for 10 minutes until the prawns are cooked. Serve immediately with freshly cooked white rice.

HOT AND SOUR MALAY FISH CURRY Ikan Asam Pedas

Fragrant and spicy, this curry is enriched with a touch of coconut milk.

Serves 4
Preparation time: 30 mins
Cooking time: 15 mins

⅓ cup (85 ml) oil
1 cm (½ in) galangal root, bruised
3–4 slices *asam gelugur* or 1½ heaped tablespoons tamarind pulp soaked in 4 tablespoons water, mashed and strained to obtain juice
2½ cups (625 ml) water
6 thick fish fillets (about 750 g/ 1½ lbs)
4 sprigs *laksa* leaves (*daun kesum*), minced
3 tablespoons thick coconut milk
2 teaspoons sugar
1 teaspoon salt
Cucumber and Pineapple Achar (page 35)

SPICE PASTE
2 candlenuts, roughly chopped
15 dried chillies, cut into lengths and soaked in warm water
10 shallots, peeled and halved
4 cloves garlic, peeled and halved
½ teaspoon turmeric powder
1 cup (250 ml) water

1. Prepare the Cucumber and Pineapple Achar by following the instructions on page 35.
2. Grind the Spice Paste ingredients to a paste in a mortar or blender, adding a little oil if necessary to keep the blades turning.
3. Heat the oil in a pot over medium heat and stir-fry the Spice Paste and galangal for 5 minutes until fragrant. Add the *asam gelugur* or tamarind juice and ½ cup (125 ml) water, and cook for 5 minutes.
4. Add the rest of the water and bring to a boil. Then add the fish, *laksa* leaves, coconut milk and season with the sugar and salt. Simmer, uncovered, for another 5 minutes until the oil separates from the coconut milk. Serve with freshly cooked white rice and a small bowl of Cucumber and Pineapple Achar on the side.

ICE KACHANG Shaved Ice with Red Beans

A delicious way to beat the heat, Ice Kachang is a mound of shaved ice piled onto a mixture of beans and jellies. A splash of brightly coloured syrup, a generous helping of evaporated milk or sweetened condensed milk and it's a treat that everyone will enjoy. Any combination of beans, fruits and jellies can be used—the ones listed here are just suggestions.

Serves 4
Preparation time: 20 mins

4 heaped tablespoons sweet red adzuki beans (see note)
4 heaped tablespoons sweet corn kernels or creamed corn
4 heaped tablespoons diced jelly in assorted colours (see note)
4 heaped tablespoons chendol jellies (optional, see note)
4 tablespoons crushed peanuts
4 teaspoons sliced preserved nutmeg fruit (optional, see note)
Shaved ice
¼ cup (60 ml) tablespoons Palm Sugar Syrup (see note on page 49)
¼ cup (60 ml) red cordial or coloured sugar syrup
½ cup (125 ml) evaporated milk or sweetened condensed milk

Divide the beans, corn kernels, jelly, *chendol*, peanuts and nutmeg fruit into 4 individual bowls. Top with a cone of shaved ice and drizzle the Palm Sugar Syrup, cordial and milk over each bowl. Serve immediately.

> **NOTE:** Sweet red adzuki beans, diced jelly and preserved nutmeg fruit are available in cans in supermarkets. Other canned fruits can also be used. *Chendol* jellies are short, green noodle-like strips made from rice flour. They are sold in packets in supermarkets. Shaved ice is absolutely necessary for this dessert; you can make it by crushing ice cubes in a food processor or blender.

GULA MELAKA Sago Pearls with Coconut Milk and Palm Sugar

Smooth sago pearls bathed in creamy coconut milk and golden brown Palm Sugar Syrup make this one of Malaysia's best-loved desserts. The name literally means "Malacca Sugar", although palm sugar (also known as *gula merah* or "red sugar") is made throughout the country.

Serves 6–8
Preparation time: 5 mins
Cooking time: 20 mins

1½ cups (150 g) dried sago pearls
¼ teaspoon pandanus extract or
   3 pandanus leaves, tied in a knot
12 cups (3 litres) water
1 cup (250 ml) Palm Sugar Syrup (see
   note on page 49)
1½ cups (375 ml) coconut cream
Mint leaves, to garnish (optional)

1. Rinse the sago pearls and place in a pot with the pandanus extract or pandanus leaves. Add the water and bring to a boil, stirring constantly for 15 minutes. If using pandanus leaves, remove and discard them. Remove the pot from the heat, cover and set aside for 5 minutes.
2. Drain the sago pearls, discarding the water. Rinse the sago under cold running water and drain again. Spoon the sago pearls into individual serving bowls and refrigerate until set.
3. To serve, drizzle the Palm Sugar Syrup and coconut cream over the sago and serve, garnished with mint leaves if desired.

SAGO WITH HONEYDEW AND COCONUT MILK

Serves 6–8
Preparation time: 25 mins
Cooking time: 15 mins

7 tablespoons dried sago pearls
9 cups (2½ litres) water
½ cup (100 g) sugar
1 ripe honeydew melon or
   cantaloupe
1½ cups (375 ml) coconut cream

1. Rinse the sago pearls, place in a pot and bring to a boil with 8 cups (2 litres) water, stirring constantly for 15 minutes. Remove the pot from the heat, cover and set aside for 5 minutes. Drain the sago pearls, discarding the water. Rinse the sago under cold running water, drain again and set aside.
2. Boil the sugar and ½ cup (125 ml) water to make a golden syrup. Remove from the heat and set aside to cool.
3. Peel the honeydew, halve, deseed, and discard the soft centre. Blend half the melon flesh in a juicer or process in a blender with ½ cup (125 ml) water. Cube the other half of the melon flesh or shape into small balls with a melon baller. Mix the cooked sago pearls, coconut cream, honeydew juice and cubes, and drizzle a little sugar syrup over to taste. Serve well chilled.

PANCAKES WITH SWEET COCONUT FILLING Kueh Dadar

A Nonya version of the Malay Kueh Dadar is often served with a coconut sauce as a teatime treat or snack, but also makes a wonderful dessert.

Makes 12 pancakes
Preparation time: 20 mins
Cooking time: 1 hour 10 mins

BATTER
1 cup (150 g) flour
¼ teaspoon salt
1 egg, lightly beaten
⅓ cup (85 ml) fresh milk
½ teaspoon pandanus or vanilla extract
1 cup (250 ml) water
2 teaspoons melted butter or oil

SWEET COCONUT FILLING
3 cups (300 g) fresh grated coconut
1½ cups ((375 ml) water
3 pandanus leaves (optional)
¼ teaspoon salt
¾ cup (150 g) palm sugar, shaved

COCONUT SAUCE
½ cup (125 ml) thick coconut milk
½ cup (125 ml) cup water
3 pandanus leaves or ¼ teaspoon pandanus extract
1 teaspoon sugar
1 teaspoon cornstarch
¼ teaspoon salt

1. First make the Batter by sifting the flour and salt together into a bowl. Add the egg, milk, pandanus extract and water, and stir until the Batter is smooth. Add the butter or oil and mix well. Cover and allow the Batter to stand for 20 to 30 minutes.

2. Place all the Sweet Coconut Filling ingredients in a saucepan and simmer over low heat, stirring occasionally, for about 30 minutes, until thick and almost dry. Be careful not to burn the sugar. Remove from the heat, transfer to a small bowl and set aside to cool. Then discard the pandanus leaves, if using.

3. Combine the Coconut Sauce ingredients in a saucepan and stir continuously over low heat for 15 minutes until the sauce thickens. Discard the pandanus leaves, if using, and strain to remove any lumps and keep aside in a warm place.

4. To cook the pancakes, grease a non-stick griddle with a little butter and spoon 3 tablespoons of the Batter onto it to make a pancake about 15–20 cm (6–8 in) in diameter. Cook over low heat until the pancake sets and browns, about 2 minutes. Flip the pancake over and cook for a few seconds. Remove from the heat and set aside on a plate. Repeat until all the Batter is used up.

5. To serve, place 2 tablespoons of the Sweet Coconut Filling on one side of each pancake, fold the sides in and roll up. Repeat until all the filling and pancakes are used used. Serve warm or at room temperature with a little Coconut Sauce drizzled on top.

> **NOTE:** The unused Batter tends to thicken as you cook the pancakes. Thin it down with a tablespoon or two of water as you go along.

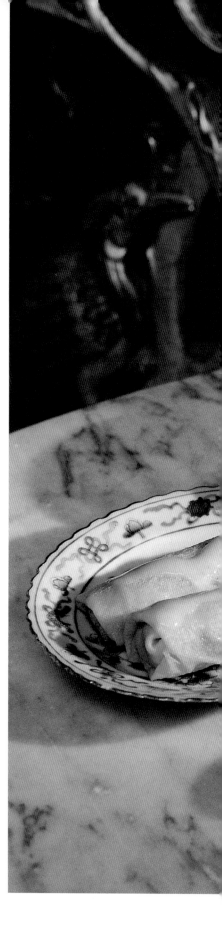

INDEX OF RECIPES

MAIL-ORDER/ONLINE SOURCES

The ingredients used in this book can be found in markets featuring the foods of Southeast Asia. Many of them can also be found in any well-stocked supermarket. Ingredients not found locally may be available from the mail-order/online addresses listed below.

USA

Asian Food Grocer
asianfoodgrocer.com
Asian Food Grocer offers a huge selection of unique Asian goods, including food, candy, beverages, household items, and more!

Bolsadeal
contact@bolsadeal.com
bolsadeal.com
We carry wholesale products from a wide variety of categories including food, groceries, beverages, household, dessert and sweet.

Dekalb Farmers Market
dekalbfarmersmarket.com
Spacious grocery store with cafeteria for organic produce & specialty foods is popular on weekends.

Essence of Thailand
essenceofthailand.com
A range of authentic Malaysian spices, sauces, and coconut milk from carefully selected and trusted brands to give you only the best when looking for must-have items for your pantry.

House of Spices
customerservice@
    houseofspicesindia.com
orders@hosindia.com
hosindia.com
From Authentic cooking ingredients to regional snacks and drinks, they have a combination of premium quality brands to suit your taste.

Just Asian Food
support@justasianfood.com
justasianfood.com
Find and buy unique Asian goods, including food, candy, beverages, household items & more!

The Spice House
support@thespicehouse.
    com
thespicehouse.com
From Adobo to Za'atar, The Spice House has every type of spice, herb, and seasoning to create exquisite flavour in all your dishes.

AUSTRALIA

Asian Grocer Online
support@asiangroceronline.
    com.au
asiangroceronline.com.au
Includes beverage, household item, fresh product, dairy, meats, snacks and more!

Asian Grocery Store
admin@AsianGroceryStore.
    com.au
asiangrocerystore.com.au
Provide high quality, rare asian food/oriental food/products and grocery.

Intradco Pty Ltd
intradco.com.au
Your local Asian grocery market.

Jackie M
jackiem.com.au
A wide range of seasonings, bottled sauces, dried food-stuffs, spices and fresh ingredients.

Just Go Shop
support@justgoshop.com.au
justgoshop.com.au
Specialise in Malaysian food products.

My Asian Grocer
myasiangrocer.com.au/
    contact/
myasiangrocer.com.au
A wide range of products from condiments to kitchenware. Stockist for Asian brands from Ayam to Yeo's.

MALAYSIA

Essential Ingredients
essentials.my/contact-us/
essentials.my
A wide range of good baking ingredients, food supplies and food ingredients.

Mak Nyonya
maknyonya.com/contact-us/
maknyonya.com
A full range and variety of instant cooking pastes and instant sauces.

Potboy Groceries
potboy.com.my/contact
potboy.com.my
An online grocer shopping destination where you can discover new brands, replenish the everyday products you love and look out for the latest must-haves.

UK

Asian Online Superstore
asian.onlineuk@gmail.com
asiangroceryuk.com
Your one-stop shop for Filipino, Thai, Malaysian, Korean, Chinese and Japanese products.

Halal Street
hello@halalstreet.co.uk
halalstreet.co.uk
The largest collection of Malaysian products in the United Kingdom.

Malaysian Food Supermarket
malaysianfoodsupermarket.
    uk
Sauce and dressings, paste and seasonings, cooking ingredients, ready meal, rice and noodle, snacks and biscuits, drinks, home baking and spreads.

Malaysian Supermarket
malaysiansupermarket.uk/
    contact/
malaysiansupermarket.uk
Halal products available here.

Melbury & Appleton
melburyandappleton.co.uk/
    customer-service-4-w.asp
melburyandappleton.co.uk
Food and ingredients for cooking Thai, Chinese, Vietnamese, Malaysian, Indonesian and Korean dishes.

Oriental Mart
sales@orientalmart.co.uk
orientalmart.co.uk
An array of Malaysian products that range from sweet treats to snack on, to essential ingredients that will help to fill your home with mouth-watering spicy and aromatic smells.

Thai Food Online
info@thai-food-online.co.uk
thai-food-online.co.uk
A variety of Malaysian cooking pastes, fruits and ingredients.

"Books to Span the East and West"

Tuttle Publishing was founded in 1832 in the small New England town of Rutland, Vermont [USA]. Our core values remain as strong today as they were then—to publish best-in-class books which bring people together one page at a time. In 1948, we established a publishing office in Japan—and Tuttle is now a leader in publishing English-language books about the arts, languages and cultures of Asia. The world has become a much smaller place today and Asia's economic and cultural influence has grown. Yet the need for meaningful dialogue and information about this diverse region has never been greater. Over the past seven decades, Tuttle has published thousands of books on subjects ranging from martial arts and paper crafts to language learning and literature—and our talented authors, illustrators, designers and photographers have won many prestigious awards. We welcome you to explore the wealth of information available on Asia at **www.tuttlepublishing.com**.

Published by Tuttle Publishing, an imprint of Periplus Editions (HK) Ltd.

www.tuttlepublishing.com

Copyright © 2022 Periplus Editions (HK) Ltd.

ISBN: 978-0-8048-5574-7

(Previously published as Authentic Recipes from Malaysia ISBN: 978-0-7946-0296-3 HC; The Food of Malaysia ISBN: 978-0-7946-0609-1 HC)

All recipes were tested in the Periplus Test Kitchen.
Photo Credits: All photography by Luca Invernizzi Tettoni. Except pages 4, 8, 9 by R. Moh'd Noh Salleh; and pages 5, 7, 19 by Jill Gocher. Endpapers: top left, Iamsom/Shutterstock.com; middle left, Abdul Razak Latif/Shutterstock.com; top right, YuriAbas/Shutterstock.com; middle right dolphfyn/Shutterstock.com; bottom right, SvetlanaSF/Shutterstock.com
Illustration: page 11 from *Kampung Boy—Yesterday and Today* by Lat.
Food Styling: pages 54, 59, 60, 65, 84 and 88 by Mrs Ong Kiat Kim and Ms Christina Ong.

Acknowledgments: The publisher would like to thank all those people who assisted in the preparation of this book. Particular thanks are due to the following Malacca stores for the loan of antiques and artifacts: Abdul Company, Fatimah Antik Stor, Malacca Junk Store and Ringo Classics & Antiques. Our sincere thanks also to Inche Mushlim Musa of Kampung Paku, Alor Gajah, and to "Madame Fatso" of Malacca's New Bunga Raya Restaurant. Thanks also to various people in Singapore who assisted by lending plates and props: Mrs Wee Kim Wee, Mrs Julie Albers and Mrs Gloria Tok.

Distributed by

North America, Latin America & Europe
Tuttle Publishing
364 Innovation Drive
North Clarendon, VT 05759-9436 U.S.A.
Tel: 1 (802) 773-8930
Fax: 1 (802) 773-6993
info@tuttlepublishing.com
www.tuttlepublishing.com

Asia Pacific
Berkeley Books Pte. Ltd.
3 Kallang Sector #04-01
Singapore 349278
Tel: (65) 6741 2178
Fax: (65) 6741 2179
inquiries@periplus.com.sg
www.tuttlepublishing.com

25 24 23 22
10 9 8 7 6 5 4 3 2 1

Printed in China   2205EP